today's menu du jour

A CHEF'S COMPANION TO MENU PLANNING & WRITING

Klaus Theyer, CCC

Kendall Hunt
publishing company

Back cover photo by Sara Martins.

Kendall Hunt
publishing company

www.kendallhunt.com
Send all inquiries to:
4050 Westmark Drive
Dubuque, IA 52004-1840

ISBN 978-0-7575-9409-0

Printed in the United States of America
10 9 8 7 6 5 4 3 2 1

Contents

Introduction

The menu, **"The Silent Salesperson,"** is likely the most important merchandising tool available to any foodservice operation. Its design and layout should attract and awaken the interest of potential customers and encourage them to become patrons.

Contrary to most other menu planning and design books, I am focusing more on the layout and on writing a menu than demographics and feasibility studies, which should be, and usually are, prepared by professionals in that field.

Through my fifty-year career as a cook, chef, catering manager, and teacher, I participated in many openings of restaurants, hotels, and catering facilities, their layout and design, freestanding or within a property. As a teacher for the last twenty-nine years, I have read many publications on this topic and used some of them for teaching students, aspiring managers, and cooks alike (chefs are cooks, too). I found that the majority of these publications focused on areas that should best be left to professionals, yet offered very limited information and examples on the essential "how to" describe menu offerings appropriately, leaving users who are in need of a quick reference without a resource.

A very personal observation: Menu writing, since its beginning, has followed rules and standards based on traditional cooking and presentation methods. Over the last twenty-five years, cooking methods, awareness of food preparation and its impact on one's health, as well as the influence of the many different cultures and their food products, have allowed chefs utilizing these methods and products to create healthier menu items.

Subsequently, the traditional presentation style has also undergone considerable changes. It is just natural progress that menu writing style, the "descriptive copy," followed the same trend, so one must remain open minded when judging the written menu. Although not all standards have gone by the wayside, they definitely have been influenced by what we have learned over the years and what the more sophisticated customer today expects to read to be stimulated and to differentiate offerings from various establishments.

After you had the opportunity to read through the book, if you have any suggestions for improving this publication or for topics you think should be covered, do not hesitate to contact me and share your thoughts.

For updates, corrections and communication, please visit my website *www.menuforprofit.com*

Your comments are welcome and appreciated.

Klaus Theyer CCC,
etservice1978@gmail.com

Acknowledgments

Today's Menu du jour could not have been written without the encouragement and support from my colleagues at Humber College.

A special "thank you" is owed to Dean Alister Mathieson, who strongly supported the project and continuously promotes the book to colleges across Canada and the United States.

I am especially thankful for the support I received from my chef colleagues, members of the Toques Blanches Toronto and the Escoffier Society of Toronto and the CCFCC, the Canadian Culinary Federation, who freely contributed, criticised, edited, and are in support of this project.

In particular, I would like to recognize the following industry colleagues and their respective companies for their contribution to this book. In fairness to all, they are listed in alphabetical order:

Bartley, Robert (Executive Chef, Maple Leaf Sports & Entertainment Ltd)
Chiaromonte, Domenic (Chef and Co-Owner of T2 Tazza Lounge)
Fernandes, Anthony (Executive Chef and Food and Beverage Director, Royal Equator Inc.)
Fischbacher, Rudi CCC (Past Chairman Canadian Culinary Institute, the education arm of the Canadian Culinary Federation, Coordinator Culinary Programs, School of Hospitality, Recreation & Tourism, Humber College)
Garcelon, David CCC (Director Culinary, the Waldorf Astoria Hotel, New York)
Gardener, Glen (Executive Chef, Sheraton Parkway Toronto North Hotel)
Glitz, Tony (Executive Chef, RS Real Sports Bar & Grill)
Jachecki, Mark CCC - ACF (Founder at Barik Consulting Inc.)
Morin, Brian CCC (Owner and Executive Chef of the Beerbistro)
Myshok, Norman CCC (Past Chairman, Canadian Culinary Institute, the education arm of the Canadian Culinary Federation, Corporate Chef, Canada Bread)
Palmer, Timothy (Restaurant Chef for the EPIC, Royal York Hotel Toronto)
Pharand-Theyer, Jeannine (Professor, School of Hospitality & Tourism Management, George Brown College)
Placko, John (Culinary Consulting, Modern Culinary Academy)
Schnell, Albert CCC (Retired, Hilton Hotels Canada & International)
Spitzer, Gerard (Retired Restaurant Critique, Montreal)
Zimmer, Hilde (Chair, School of Hospitality & Tourism Management, George Brown College)
Zyvatkauskas, Raimund A. CCC (Executive Chef, Kingbridge Conference Centre & Institute)

I would be remiss not to thank Pat Cuda from *Humber College* and Richard Ludlow from *Kendall Hunt Publishing Company* for their advice and input, Arthur Serwaczak from *ebound* for patiently making ongoing changes to the support web-site www.menuforprofit.com, and my wife Jeannine, for contributing the catering content and the service style section, assisting with the chef's interviews, and graciously accepting the lack of focused attention during the writing of this book.

Klaus Theyer CCC

A Letter From a Friend

What I Expect from a Menu
Gerard Spitzer*

1. The menu should be written in the language used by the clientele and personnel. Many times French or other language terminology is used and is often full of translation and/or spelling mistakes.
2. There should be no professional or invented terminology. The customer shouldn't need a culinary dictionary or education to decipher the menu.
3. The menu should not be pages long with hundreds of propositions. One will immediately start to wonder whether the ingredients in the kitchen are fresh. I prefer a short menu, with daily and weekly specials.
4. A clear explanation of each dish, including the manner in which it is prepared and the basic ingredients.
5. The menu has to respect the ingredients listed, meaning that a gambas is not a small shrimp and veal scallopini is not made with turkey or pork, or a "coq au Chambertin" is not made with chicken in house wine.
6. Avoid any menu that is pompous and too difficult to understand. A menu should be simple and clear. Canned tuna will always remain canned tuna no matter how it is prepared.
7. Avoid the abusive use of different cuisines, as can be seen, for example, too many times in fusion dishes. The menu can be creative without falling into this trap.
8. I like when local specialities or food products are mentioned (eventually with the name of the producers). Organic products and special needs dishes such as vegetarian, gluten, or dairy free should be mentioned. It helps everyone at the table choose an appropriate dish.
9. Regarding plate presentation, it should be simple. Avoid too much decoration. The main ingredients of the dish you have chosen should be clearly visible, and it should be clear that what you have ordered is what is on your plate.

**Gerard Spitzer studied at the School of Hotel Administration of Glion (Switzerland) and Cornell (USA). He wrote restaurant reviews during ten years for European and North American publications.*

A Menu's Job Description and Why Do We Eat?

Chapter 1

A Menu's Job Description

Besides being decorative and interesting (the cover needs to entice potential customers to read on), menus are expected to be excellent merchandising tools.

During a regular workweek, sometimes all seven days of a week, for breakfast, lunch, and dinner, a menu is expected to quietly but affirmatively point to the available offerings and may highlight the profitable ones from soup to dessert, from water(s) to eau de vie (water of life), from specialty items to complete packages, like a travel guide, but for palatable pleasures.

Over and above the above (pardon the pun), the successful menu is expected to have a clean appearance, reflecting the sanitary standard of the establishment. It must be of durable texture (lots of customer contact) and display good phraseology. (Not everyone who is hungry holds a degree in English or other foreign languages.)

Before applying for the job of "menu," you should be aware that you may be handled, used, even abused, by human beings of all ages. You may be praised for your appearance by some and criticized by others. Sometimes you may even be kidnapped by collectors, or worse, be used as evidence in a courtroom (menu writing law).

Therefore, only serious candidates need apply!
Preference is given to those who are unbiased, politically correct, picturesque, confident, and eloquent at the same time, and who will conform to every potential customer's expectation.

Good luck and Bon appétit

Dear reader,

The following description and explanation of "four menu courses" are designed in a similar format as pages of a menu, providing a summary introduction to what you can expect from the content of the book.

Bon appétit!

First Course: The Right Customer

The "right customer" is the person entering the establishment knowing what to expect. This can easily be achieved by having the exterior appearance reflected in the theme and style of the establishment.

Posting the food and beverage menu, or selected offerings, and clearly displaying selling prices will allow the potential customer to make an informed decision. Selected photos of the interior will also help to promote the establishment and, hopefully, encourage walk-ins.

It can be an uncomfortable, and perhaps an embarrassing, experience for a customer to be guided to a table, seated, but upon receiving the menu, realize that the prices are out of his or her price range, or that the menu offerings do not meet his or her expectations. A customer's comfort zone can easily be defiled for a number of reasons, which include unexpected, or lack of, desired offerings, a menu that is too expensive, the decor and seating arrangements not conforming to the customer's expectation, or the customer is uncomfortable with the appearance and demeanour of the staff. However, if the customer makes an informed choice of entering the establishment and is satisfied with the "total dining experience," then the establishment may have gained a repeat customer—the backbone of most foodservice business.

Second Course: Carefully Selected Menu Offerings Appealing and Profitable

The menu offerings must reflect the theme and concept of the establishment. The menu must be written in easily understood, yet descriptive, words that reflect quality and standards so that the potential customers can form a picture of the offerings in their minds. A selection of staple offerings, daily specials, and seasonal market-fresh products will help to convince a potential customer to become a buying customer. Statistically, a customer who has received more than, or at least what was expected, will come back.

From an operator's perspective, it is important that ingredients can be used in more than one menu offering and that the cost—selling price—gross profit margin ratio is adequate to make the desired net profit. In order to achieve this, special attention must be given to the labour cost incurred in preparing menu items.

Third Course: Product and Staff Management

As previously mentioned, an establishment must reflect in its makeup the operating philosophy of management by being able to convey, through minimal wording, the concept and style of the establishment.

First impressions—cleanliness, welcoming appearance, professionalism, meeting expected quality—are catch phrases for applied standards. Most commonly, standards are established for quality and quantity, and standards must be set for purchasing, service, food, beverage, appearance, sales, cost and profit, reporting, communication with customer and staff, just to name a few. Then it is essential to select and hire staff that is either experienced or trainable. Each area of an establishment should have a professional and accountable individual managing the product and staff. This can only be achieved if every employee clearly understands the philosophy and standards of the establishment and receives appropriate training.

Fourth Course: Optimum Sale, Superb Service, Satisfied Customers, and Profit

Usually the last course consumed is cheese, fruit, dessert, coffee, or teas, which are very important menu offerings. Most customers will remember highlights of the consumed goods, and especially the last items they had, including coffee or tea. These must be freshly prepared, satisfying, and provide a memorable ending to a great lunch or dinner for the customer.

Operators who follow the principles of profitable menu planning, an important part of the business plan, place highly profitable menu offerings strategically on the menu, train staff to optimize sales by promoting profitable items, and are able to satisfy customers. These operators will enjoy repeat customers and profitability.

"The pleasures of the table are of all times and all ages,
of every country and every day."

A quote from Jean Anthelme Brillat-Savarin (1755–1826)
A famous French gourmet and renowned writer.
His work consists of *La Physiologie du Goût* (*The Physiology of Taste*)

The "IDEAL" Menu for Financial Success in Foodservice Das "Über" Menu

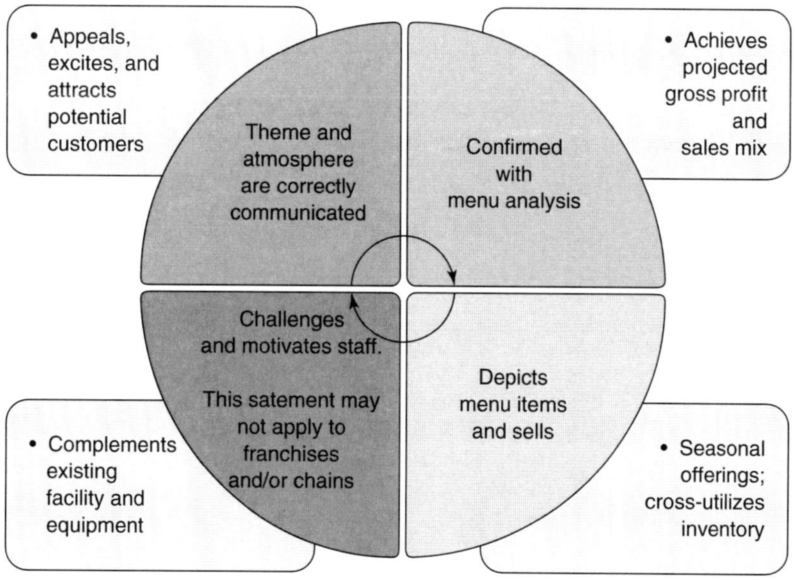

Why Do We Eat?

Understanding *why we eat and what we eat* should guide us in determining what we write on the menu.

There are very important reasons for eating:

- To sustain life
- Building bodies and minds—physiological and nutritional needs
- To socialize—to civilize
- To see and to be seen
- For religious reasons
- To explore and learn
- For the "feel-good factor"

and many more equally important different occasions:

- Family meals
- Social gatherings
- Celebrations
- Weddings
- Grieving
- Farewells
- Religious events
- Ethnic traditions
- Business negotiations
- Hosting dignitaries
- Demonstration of wealth

Each occasion has its own written or unwritten "personalized menu."

These offered menu choices will be strongly influenced by the occasion's type; however, there are other influencing factors: the sensory properties of foods and accompanying beverages, such as taste, smell, temperature, and presentation/appearance.

Social, emotional factors, such as concerns about likes and dislikes, awareness and attitudes related to diets and health, are also influencing factors. Personal beliefs and values about issues such as organic or genetically modified foods, fresh or preserved foods, or diet-specific selections may be important for some individuals.

Other factors, such as cultural, religious, and economic factors also strongly influence our choices. Education, ethnic origin, seasonality, and prices of products play a major role in our food choice.

As a menu writer, one must be sensitive to these situations, be able to communicate the evoked feelings, be familiar with the availability of required products, and have the necessary facilities and skilled staff to carry out a personalized special occasion menu.

Menu Concept Considerations: Fads and Trends

Chapter 2

In Perspective; What is a Menu?

A menu is a summary of available selections. When one refers to a menu, it is usually in conjunction with food and beverage; however, the word *menu* is used for many other applications from computer programs, to cell phones, to company's switchboards, to foodservice facilities. All of the beforementioned offer verbal or written choices, based on prescribed functionality or your needs and likings.

> ***The Menu should Guide the Reader in a Predetermined Direction***
>
> *In a restaurant a menu is most often presented as printed media; it can also be presented verbally. The printed media is often on public display, internally and/or externally, as a listing of available options for a potential customer to select from.*

Depiction—Depicted Menu

Depiction is the process of the mind's converting written or verbal expressions (words) into a pictorial equivalence or a representation of forms or objects on a surface by means of lines or drawings of conceptions.

Themes and Concepts

The Process of Establishing Themes and Concepts

Basically there are three types of restaurants:

1. **Fast food or quick service**—Offering limited menu items that can be prepared quickly. These locations often feature eat-in and take-out areas and drive-thru windows.

2. **Mid-scale or family type**—Offering full meals at a medium price that customers perceive as "good value." They can be full service, buffets, or limited service establishments with customers ordering at the counter and having their food brought to them.
3. **Upscale or fine dining**—Offering high-quality cuisine at high-end prices. They usually provide well-trained service staff, a maître d', often a sommelier, and a high quality of ambience.

What kind/type of restaurant to open is a complex decision, based on many factors:

How does this establishment fit into your or the corporate business plan? What are the primary focuses?
What are the goals and objectives?
Should it be part of a chain or have its own identity, franchised or sole proprietor?
Should it be unique, or extravagant, or exclusive, or should it accommodate the majority of potential customers based on demographics?

Once these important decisions have been made, everything that follows will need to conform: the dining room layout and design, the kitchen and bar, catering and takeout, type of menu(s), and the number of people needed to cover all positions and shifts.

Many things need to be decided upon manifesting your restaurant's concept. Perhaps an important question to ask is: What kind of restaurant would I want to eat in every day? The final selection of the concept must instill confidence and comfort in you, investors, suppliers, and all other creditors.

An equally important question to ask is: What kind of restaurant is sustainable in this demographic area? Most populated areas have established restaurants; subsequently, there is competition. The type of competition identified through a **competitive analysis** might be difficult to avoid altogether, so perhaps the best way to beat the competition is to offer something different.

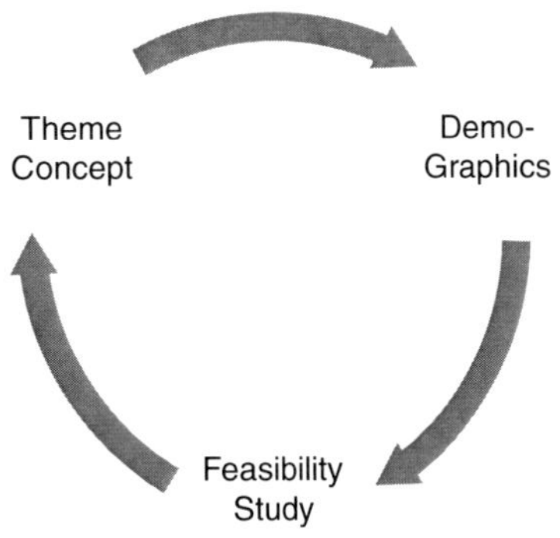

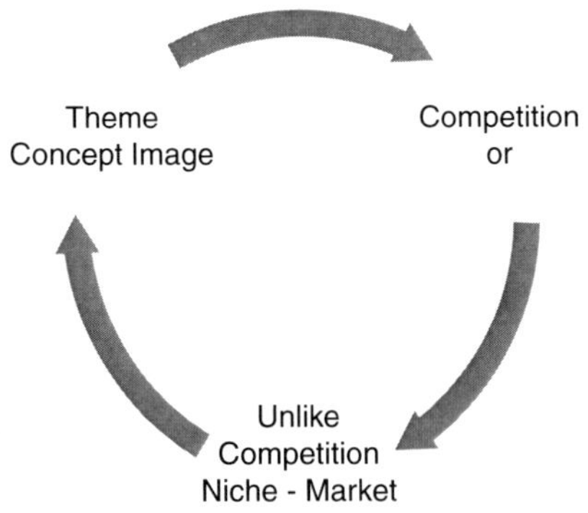

Instead of opening a Chinese or Thai restaurant, perhaps a Malaysian or Vietnamese theme would not be a **head–on competition**, yet it potentially would attract the same clientele as the Chinese or Thai establishment.

Another example: If there is a strong presence of already competing Italian restaurants, considering a Mediterranean restaurant encompassing specialities from all the Mediterranean countries, would be different enough not to be a head-on-competition and would possibly attract a larger cluster of potential customers.

Menu Concept Considerations

The Potential Customer Base

Downtown office employees will most likely go to a nearby place for lunch but will eat dinner in the area where they live or go home to come back to the city for an evening out.

Suburban residents will most likely be going to town (suburban downtown area or next larger city's downtown) for an evening out but will stay in the neighbourhood for an everyday meal.

The Type of Eatery

Is there a need or sensible reason to have one or all of the various licences to serve alcoholic beverages? Will the type of customer you are serving be able to drink alcoholic beverages: office workers, students, adolescents, families? Is the eatery specialized through its appearance, type, or style to serve a specific type of customer? Consider whether to open a fast food, fine dining, family type, tourist attraction, catering, or institutional establishment.

Atmosphere

The theme and concept, its makeup, and menu must be a reflection of the atmosphere or, in reverse, must create an atmosphere.

Customers will have a perception prior to entering the establishment of what they should expect based on the name, makeup, advertising, and decor of the building. Subsequent to entering, they will either be neutral, satisfied, pleasantly surprised, or disappointed.

Their expectations of the offerings documented on the menu(s), the personality of the staff, followed by the quality, taste, and presentation of the menu items and the availability of appropriately matching beverage selection and the perceived value of this expectation will further influence their feelings of neutrality, satisfaction, pleasant surprise or disappointment.

Labour Requirement

As previously mentioned, the type of establishment and the result of a feasibility study will ultimately determine the requirements for labour. Should the open positions be staffed by trained, qualified, and experienced staff or are trainable and inexperienced workers sufficient?

The type of eatery does commit to a certain level of service and staffing that customers expect, from someone who flips hamburgers to an executive chef who directs a brigade of chefs and cooks, from counter or buffet service to tableside cooking, from a beverage menu to a sommelier. In each situation there is a tremendous difference in training, qualifications, expertise, and subsequent remuneration.

Development Cost

Although it is not within the purview of this book, I do want to mention that the type of eatery will strongly determine the business costs, as well as the cost of developing that business. If it is a franchise, the popularity of the franchise sometimes outvalues the structural cost, meaning that it might be less costly to build the actual building than to purchase the franchise rights, including the theme, concepts, its popularity, and perceived future earning power.

Concept Checklist

A restaurant concept is the result of combined characteristics:

- Physical establishment; type of eatery
- Type of potential customer
- Unrestricted menus vs. limited menus
- Eat in, take out, delivered
- Catering, in house, on location, personal chef services
- Atmosphere
- Level of service and expertise

Just a Few More Considerations

Your *concept* should be different enough to clearly separate your idea from the competition.

The clarity of your concept is very important. If your concept is not understood or sounds too extravagant or out-of-place, it may not attract the customers you would like to have.

Introducing a new concept can be very expensive in advertising costs, and it may take longer than anticipated for customers to buy into that concept.

Great care must be taken when pricing your menu items. Competition indirectly dictates the menu prices, and unless your dishes are quite different than the competitors', potential customers may not be prepared to pay more than what the competition is charging.

A menu must be designed with attractive and popular menu items that should be easily cross-utilized to minimize waste and limit the need to store a great variety of different products. Every perishable product purchased ideally should be able to be utilized in at least two different menu offerings or menu items that differentiate themselves through diverse cooking methods. The same raw product should transform into different dishes using a variety of cooking methods.

Additionally, offered menu items should be priced not only on product cost but also considering the actual labour involvement. From a labour perspective, it is a lot cheaper to grill a steak than to prepare an open-faced sandwich, but a steak will yield a much higher selling price.

Available equipment should be considered when planning menu items so that equipment and workspace is available, fully utilized, and not overloaded. Overloading equipment could cause delays in preparation and unexpected waiting time for customers. For example. offering "au gratin" dishes without a salamander could cause considerable problems.

You researched the concept, evaluated all considerations, did your feasibility study, and are ready to settle for a specific location when your real estate broker calls you with a new listing he received, a great restaurant opportunity, in a great location in a high traffic area that you previously did not consider. You must ensure that your concept is compatible with this new location. If the population in this new area is different than the assessed area, you should obtain new demographic data to verify that your concept will still work or make the necessary changes.

The Concept and You

You must be comfortable with all aspects of the selected concept. If there are any doubts, change it before you implement it. Any change after implementation has a pricetag attached to it, which could be quite hefty (advice from personal experience). If you are in a partnership, do not rely overly on the ambition, taste, and skills of the partner(s). Everyone involved should be readily replaceable; otherwise, ideas may vanish if a partner(s) becomes unavailable and all the work you have put in may be lost.

Fads and Trends - Should Be Evaluated Carefully

A **trend** is usually for the long term, the general direction in which something tends to move; it can also be a successful fad.

A **fad** is short term, something that is adopted with great enthusiasm for a brief period of time, but then lost popularity and did not become a trend.

Although responding to or creating fads and trends shows that you're aware of what is current in the industry and what consumers are looking for. handle this with caution since fads have a tendency to be around only for a short while and trends take time to establish and prove themselves. Since food trends influence food selection, food service, and food presentation, the chef and foodservice staff, as well as the consumers, need to be able to quite easily understand the meaning, since no one likes to admit ignorance because of inexperience or lack of sophistication. This should not discourage you from trying new concepts that you may have seen through your travels, but make you aware of potential pitfalls.

Then there are trends that are demographically generated: In Europe and in North America the majority of the population are "baby boomers," and their demand on and for foodservice is very different from the demand of the generation (at least two by now) that followed.

Current and Past Fads/Trends

Acid and alkaline balance

Value meals; monies spent on foodservice

Food safety

100-mile rule (supplies and purchasing)

Locally/regionally grown or raised

The carbon footprint consideration

Molecular gastronomy or molecular cuisine (Italian government legislated against molecular cuisine)

Additives (natural or chemical)

Slow food and sous-vide (under vacuum) cooking

Organic

Free range

(Continued)

Grass fed

Nostalgic and super premium

Televised cooking shows

Exotic salts and seasoning

Heart Smart (replaced by general acceptance of healthier cooking methods, styles, and products including avoidance of transfats)

In October 2009, the National Restaurant Association (USA) (NRA) surveyed more than 1,600 professional chefs, who ranked over 200 foods/menu items as "hot trends," "yesterday's news," or "perennial favorites" (or, as we like to say in Canada, "favourites"). *Four trends cracked the 80% mark*:

1. Locally grown produce (89%)
2. Bite-size/mini desserts (83%)
3. Organic produce (82%)
4. Nutritionally balanced children's dishes (81%)

And this just in: Mark Zuckerberg, the founder of Facebook, stated publicly that he is only eating meat from animals he killed himself as part of a sustainable living project. Working together with well-known chef Jesse Cool, he humanely killed a pig and a goat. Apparently his first kill for food was a lobster, which he boiled alive, followed by a chicken, which he ate including edible entrails. Could that be the beginning of a fad?

Excerpts from the Canadian Restaurant Foodservice Chefs' Surveys of 2010 and 2011

Excerpt from the Canadian Restaurant Foodservice 2010 Chef's survey based on responses from nearly 400 professional chefs published by the Canadian Restaurant Foodservice Association:

> *The Chef's Survey in cooperation with the Canadian Culinary Federation (CCFCC) was conducted by independent market research firm Brand Spark International between January and February, 2010. Chefs were asked to rate the popularity of a variety of menu items and cooking methods, identifying hot trends, up-and comers, perennial favourites and yesterday's news.*

Partially reprinted with permission. To purchase a copy of the full report, visit www.crfa.ca/research.

Top 10: Hot Trends

1. Locally sourced foods
2. Sustainability
3. Organics
4. Artisanal cheeses
5. Simplicity/back to basics
6. Nutritional/healthy cuisine
7. Free-range poultry/pork
8. Small plates/tapas/mezze/dim sum
9. Bite size/mini desserts
10. Superfruits (e.g., acai, goji berry, mangosteen)

Hot Trends—Menu Trends

1. Small plates / tapas / mezza / dim sum
2. Inexpensive/underused cuts of meat (e.g., beef cheeks, brisket, pork shoulder, skirt steak)
3. Half portions/smaller portions for smaller price
4. Specialty/gourmet sandwiches
5. Gourmet burgers/build-your-own burgers

Hot Trends—Preparation Methods

1. Sous vide
2. Liquid nitrogen chilling / freezing
3. Smoking
4. Braising
5. Cooking with tea

Top 10 Up and Comers

1. Ancient grains (e.g., kamut, spelt, amaranth)
2. Gluten-free beer
3. Vegan entrees
4. Organic alcohol
5. African cuisine
6. New/fabricated cuts of meat
7. Gluten-free cuisine
8. Middle Eastern cuisine
9. Quinoa
10. Nontraditional fish (e.g., branzino [European or Mediterranean sea bass], Arctic char, barram-undi (farmed fish from Australia)

Up and Comers—Menu Trends

1. Vegan entrees
2. Meatless/vegetarian entree

(Continued)

3. Half portions/smaller portions for smaller price
4. Inexpensive/underused cuts of meat (e.g., beef cheeks, brisket, pork shoulder, skirt steak)
5. Low-calorie/low-fat entrees

Up and Comers—Preparation Methods

1. Cooking with tea
2. Liquid nitrogen chilling/freezing
3. Sous vide
4. Pickling
5. Oil-poaching confit

Top 10 Perennial Favourites

1. Chocolate desserts
2. Shrimp
3. Chicken
4. Pasta
5. Shellfish
6. Scallops
7. Italian
8. Hot soup
9. Searing / sautéing
10. Lobster

Top 10 Yesterday's News

1. Ostrich/emu
2. Cupcakes
3. Gazpacho/cold soups
4. Kobe beef (Wagyu)
5. Foams
6. Bottled water
7. Frying
8. Mexican-inspired entree salads
9. Couscous
10. Tilapiaundi; Micro-distilled/Artisan liquor; Meatless/Vegetarian entrees.

Excerpt from the Canadian Restaurant Foodservice 2011 Chef's survey based on more than 500 professional chefs published by the Canadian Restaurant Foodservice Association:

The Chef's survey in cooperation with the Canadian Culinary Federation (CCFCC) was conducted by independent market research firm Brand Spark International between January and February, 2011. Chefs were asked to rate the popularity of a variety of menu items and cooking methods, identifying hot trends, up-and-comers, perennial favourites, and yesterday's news.

Partially reprinted with permission. To purchase a copy of the full report, visit www.crfa.ca/research.

Top 10 Hot Trends

1. Locally produced foods and locally inspired dishes
2. Sustainability
3. Nutritional and health
4. Organic
5. Simplicity/back to basics
6. Gluten-free/food allergy conscious
7. Craft beer/microbrews
8. Artisanal cheeses
9. Bite size/mini desserts
10. Quinoa/ancient grains

Hot Trends—Menu Trends

1. Locally inspired dishes
2. Specialty/gourmet sandwiches
3. Low-calorie/low-fat entrees
4. Inexpensive/underused cuts of meat
5. Half portions/smaller portions for smaller price

Hot Trends—Preparation Methods

1. Smoking
2. Sous vide
3. Braising
4. Liquid nitrogen chilling/freezing
5. Cooking with tea

Top 10 Up and Comers

1. Gluten-free beer
2. African cuisine
3. Red rice
4. Organic wine/beer/liquor/cocktails
5. Peruvian cuisine
6. New/fabricated cuts of meat
7. Cooking with tea
8. Beer sommeliers/Cicerones
9. Culinary cocktails
10. Traditional ethnic desserts (e.g., delimanjoo, flan, qatayef)

Up and Comers—Menu Trends

1. Inexpensive/underused cuts of meat (e.g., beef cheeks, brisket, pork shoulder, skirt steak)
2. Vegetarian entrees
3. Half portions/smaller portions for smaller price

(Continued)

4. *Fancy/gourmet fast food*
5. *Meatless/vegetarian entrees*

Up and Comers—Preparation Methods

1. *Cooking with tea*
2. *Liquid nitrogen chilling/freezing*
3. *Pickling*
4. *Sous vide*
5. *Oil-poaching/confit*

Top 10 Perennial Favourites *(Perennial favourites are items that are always popular and are long-time menu favourites)*

1. *Chocolate desserts*
2. *Cold appetizer salads*
3. *Fresh fruit*
4. *Classic desserts*
5. *Pie*
6. *Tuna*
7. *Aged meats*
8. *Carbonated beverages/soft drinks*
9. *Barbeque items*
10. *Marinades/rubs*

Top 10 Yesterday's News *(The menu items that have declined in popularity)*

1. *Gazpacho/cold soups*
2. *Tilapia*
3. *Mini-burgers*
4. *Kobe beef*
5. *Flavoured/enhanced water*
6. *Foams*
7. *Ready to serve*
8. *Catfish*
9. *Cupcakes*
10. *Energy drinks*

There are some other trends, not affecting food production as such, but becoming increasingly important in the hospitality/accommodation industry:

Cloud computing: Years ago, to place your lunch order by fax was a technological marvel. Today, with the Internet you can book, order, and pay online. All you have to do is go and eat in person or have it delivered.

American Express (Amex) unveiled "telepresence" and high-end virtual meeting options. What used to be teleconferences are now becoming virtual meetings for which rooms and foodservice are needed. All needed equipment is available for lease or purchase.

In my research on food trends I came across an interesting site/link from the government of Alberta that I would like to share with you:
http://www1.agric.gov.ab.ca/$department/deptdocs.nsf/all/sis8735

Looking Back to Look Forward: Important History and Future

Chapter 3

The following image is a scan of a **Prix Fixe Menu/Special Occasion Menu** from the Lotus Club, New York City, March 4, 1893.

Courtesy of the Library of Congress

One of the first menus composed by Georges August Escoffier was dated December 16, 1897. Here are the original handwritten version, typed text, and the English translation.

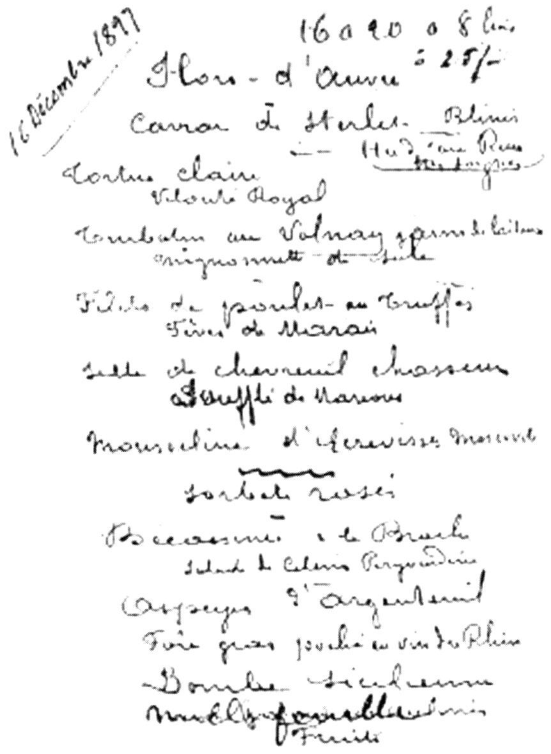

16 Décembre 1897

Hors d'œuvres

Caviar de st. Arles blinis
Tortue Claire
Veloute royal
Turbotin au Volnay garni de laitue
Vinaigrette et huile
Filet de poulet aux truffes
Fèves des marais
Selle de chevreuil chasseur
Soufflé de marrons
Mousseline d'écrevisses muscovite
Sorbet rose
Bécassine à la broche
Salade de céleri périgourdine
Asperges d'Argenteuil
Foie gras poche au vin du Rhin

Bombe Sicilienne
Mille feuilles
Fruits

December 16, 1897

Appetizers

Blinis with St. Arles caviar
Clear turtle soup
Royal cream
Turbot poached in Volnay region wine,
garnished with lettuce, vinaigrette, and oil
Filet of chicken with truffles
Broad beans
Saddle of venison hunter style
Chestnut soufflé
Crayfish mousse with Muscovy sauce
Pink sorbet
Grilled snipe
Celeriac salad périgourdine style (with truffles)
Argenteuil region asparagus
Goose liver poached in Rhine wine

Sicilian ice cream bombe
Mille-feuille pastry
Selection of fruits

A Short History of Restaurants and the Origin of the Menu

The word *menu*, describing the media that is used to list the dishes to be served in the specific order of their consumption for a defined occasion, originated in France.

The main purpose of the menu was communicate to the kitchen and banquet staff, including servers and wine waiters, the sequence of dishes to be prepared and served. When the functionality of the menu was fully realized, it was also used for the consumers as guide, and over the years evolved into the informative advertising media as it is used today.

The word *menu* itself is derived from Latin *minutus*, something made small, detailed.

The original menus in the 1600s offered consumers choices that were produced on chalkboard-easels or a placard. In French, *carte* also referred to as *escriteau*, in English, a "bill of fare."

Originally, the bills of fare were working menus used to instruct the kitchen on what to produce and the front of the house staff to select the appropriate dishes and decor to complement the meal.

While researching several books on culinary history, I concluded that all writers in principle agree on which were the first establishments using the name *restaurant*, but with slight variations.

To determine who is right, you should read the facts and believe what sounds most believable to you. At this point, almost 300 years after the fact, it does not seem possible to provide proof of who is right and who is not.

A restaurant is commonly known as a place that serves food and beverage to the general public, whereas a bar would be specialising mainly in beverages and in the past was restricted to males. Females were either not allowed or allowed only in the company of a male.

Boulanger, around 1765, is commonly credited as the Parisian bouillon (soup) vendor who set up a shop near the Louvre displaying the following signage: "Boulanger sells restoratives fit for the gods." According to *The New Larousse Gastronomique,*" first published in Paris, France in 1966 (a book I believe every culinarian should have), the sign announced "Boulanger sells magical restoratives" and elaborated on that statement by stating the following Culinary Latin words: *Venite ad me; vos qui stomach laboratis et ego restaurabo vos.* Translated into common English, this means: "If you have an upset stomach, I will restore it here."

Boulanger was limited to selling soups since he was not a member of the "Corporation of traiteurs" who were able to cook meat dishes.

The following statement is based on an article from the London newspaper *The Telegraph*, published on September 3, 2000:

> According to the *Guide Gourmand de la France*, Boulanger's restaurant was located on the corner of Rue du Louvre (then known as Rue Pouille) and Rue Bailleul. The Cafe du Musée now stands on the site, selling hot dogs and ice creams.

However, according to Rebecca L. Spang, it may not have been Boulanger, but Mathurin Roze de Chantoiseau in Paris, around 1766, who was the forgotten inventor of the first restaurant. Mathurin Roze de Chantoiseau was the son of a landowner and merchant who moved to Paris in the early 1760s.

> A third option is Beauvilliers, around 1782:
> It seems that the first Parisian restaurant worthy of the name was the one founded by Beauvilliers in 1782 in the Rue de Richelieu, called the Grande Taverne de Londres. Beauvilliers introduced the novelty of listing the dishes available on a card and serving them at small individual tables during set hours.

All history books and historians seem to agree that the first restaurants were established in France toward the end of the eighteenth century. At that time, with the exception of inns, which were primarily for travelers and street kitchens, nowhere else in Europe could one purchase a meal outside the home. Essentially, places where alcoholic beverages were sold were equipped to serve simple, inexpensive dishes either cooked on the premises or ordered from a nearby inn, bakery, or food shop, along with wine, beer, and spirits, which constituted the bulk of their business. Such tavern-restaurants existed not only in France but also in other countries. In Germany, Austria, and Alsace, Brauereien (breweries) and Weinstuben (vintners and wineries serving their own wines to the public) also served delicatessen, sauerkraut, and cheese. In Spain bodegas (wineries) served tapas. Greek taverns served various foods made with, or marinated/preserved in olive oil, as well as a variety of fortifying dishes such as stews, meat with sauce, and organ meats.

All of these places were suited to serving plain and simple fare rather than more elaborate culinary creations. For a full meal as compared to individual dishes one had to look either to a good inn or go to a *rôtisseur* or *traiteur* (caterer, from the Italian *trattorie*).

In France, these two, rôtisseur and traiteur (guilds/trade association), together with the *charcutiers,* had been granted a monopoly on all cooked meat other than pâtés, which only chefs were allowed to make.

French chef Jean-Joseph Clause is credited for creating and popularizing pâté de foie gras in 1779. Chef Clause's culinary creation was rewarded a gift of twenty pistols by King Louis XVI, and he obtained a patent for the dish in 1784. He went on to begin his own business specializing in supplying pâté to the gentry (people of high social class). By 1827, Strasberg was known as the goose-liver capital of the world.

The French Law and Pâté de Foie Gras

French law requires at least 80 percent of pâté de foie gras (goose liver pate) must be the liver. Mousse, or purée de foie gras, contains even less, 55 percent. Although other pâtés can be served warm or hot, the delicate texture of foie gras melts too easily, so pâté de foie gras should be served chilled.

Only common people actually ate in the traiteur's (butcher-delicatessen) shop, perhaps seated at a table reserved for guests in some establishments. Even a moderately well-to-do person would have preferred to order food delivered to a private home or a room at an inn or hotel or an elegant salon rented for the occasion.

Ever since the late Middle Ages the word *restaurant* had been used to describe any of a variety of rich bouillons made with chicken, beef, roots of one sort or another, onions, herbs, and, according to some recipes, spices, crystallized sugar, toasted bread, barley, butter, and even exotic ingredients.

Based on *The Rise of the Restaurant: Food: a Culinary History,* by Jean-Louis Flandrin and Massimo Montanari, Boulanger wrote on his sign: "Boulanger sells restoratives fit for the gods." This was the first restaurant in the modern sense of the term. Boulanger was followed by Roze and Pontaille, who in 1766 opened "La maison de santé" (house of health). The first Parisian restaurant worthy of the name was the one founded by Beauvilliers in 1782 called the Grande Taverne de Londres. As previously mentioned, he introduced the novelty of listing the dishes available on a menu and served them at small individual tables during fixed hours. Following the revolution, the abolition of the guilds and their privileges made it easier to open a restaurant. Cooks and servants from the great houses out of a job because their aristocratic owners had fled took advantage of the opportunity and opened restaurants and eateries. The arrival of numerous provincials in Paris, who had no family in the capital, created a pool of faithful customers, enlarged by the journalists and businessmen. It was during that time restaurants became an established institution.

According to britishmuseum.org, Cooking in Roman Britain (about fourth century CE) was often done over charcoal fires on raised hearths. An iron grate was positioned over the fire and the pan or pot placed on top. This ornate stand featured a ring, allowing it to be hung up when not in use.

And according to the Roman Cookery Museum (museums.ncl.ac.uk), wealthy Romans ate delicacies like flamingos, snails, and stuffed dormice. These were often served with a strong fish sauce called garum. In the spacious and well-equipped kitchens of nobles, numerous men, in a strict hierarchy, busied themselves: chefs, "spit-masters" responsible for roasts, and soup and sauce cooks, each accountable for his food preparations as well as his expenses. They were assisted by a swarm of kitchen boys.

According to softcafe.com, the first American restaurant to use printed menus was Delmonico's Steak House in New York City in 1837. In 1838 their menu had grown to 100 pages.

Delmonico's, opened in 1837 as America's first fine-dining restaurant, continues to serve the connoisseur of fine American food in its premier location at 56 Beaver Street, the heart of Manhattan's financial district. This was the birthplace of the Delmonico steak, Delmonico potatoes, eggs benedict, lobster newburg, and baked Alaska. The original Delmonico's offered unheard of luxury—the availability of private dining rooms, an extensive wine cellar, innovative cuisine, and, above all, warm, personal service.

Looking Forward

What Will the Future Bring? by John Placko

The principal questions, What is cooking and what does cooking do to food?, in the past was most likely responded to with the following statements:

It is the process of applying heat to convert inedible raw products into a cooked products and subsequently making them edible.

In greater detail, one would add that heat solidifies proteins, caramelizes sugars and starches. In that process flavours will be altered and liquids will evaporate.

We also know that freezing has effects on food: solidifying moist particles and liquids and/or drying products composed of solids and liquids.

Chefs all over the world use the appearance, the taste, the smell, and the sizzle of the converted product to describe what the customer will be receiving on his or her plate when ordering a certain dish from the menu.

A few years ago, a new dimension was added to the meaning of cooking: molecular cuisine—the systematic scientific study of cooking, as Klaus calls it; the alteration of the product molecule using nontraditional cooking methods.

At first, this area of study did not attract a lot of followers. But once chefs realized the immense possibilities of using and applying the findings of these studies to the possible enhancements to their daily menus, interest in this science grew quickly. Today, several well-known chefs have embraced molecular gastronomy to create delicious dishes prepared from common ingredients, yet these dishes are very different in their appearance from what the general public, our customers, are traditionally used to.

Consider a nitro-scrambled egg-and-bacon ice cream. To some of us it may sound far-fetched and perhaps not very appetizing, whereas to the adventurous, it is sought-after delicacy.

Breakfast Deconstructed

A normal breakfast offering on a menu might look like this:

Eggs any style with bacon, sautéed mushrooms, grilled tomato, toast of your choice garnished with parsley.

Here's a modern version of a breakfast plate using sous-vide, agar gel, and maltodextrin to enhance the preparations:

Warm parsley gel topped with a sous-vide cooked egg, king oyster mushroom slices, toasted baguette, seared cherry tomatoes with bacon rashers and bacon snow.

With anything new, it is important to its success that it is properly marketed. As chefs, our main marketing tool is our menu: The way we describe a dish is what will make a customer decide to order it or not.

Klaus had asked mae to provide an example of describing an item to be posted on a menu in the traditional way and after conversion. The following is simple example based on a lemon meringue pie:

Lemon Meringue Pie: a short-crust pastry shell filled with lemon curd and baked with a meringue, served with whipped cream.

A new version of the dessert that's individually plated would be described as:

Deconstructed Lemon Meringue Pie

Sugar-dusted short-crust pastry crumbs, lemon curd, blowtorch glazed meringue, and carbonated mango cubes.

About John Placko

I've worked in Canada for the past seventeen years with various organizations: Cara Operations Ltd, Prime Restaurants Inc, Campbell Company of Canada, and most recently completed three years as Director of Culinary Excellence at Maple Leaf Foods. ThinkFOOD! centre.

Prior to Canada, I worked in hotels, airline and contract catering, as well as restaurants.

My culinary competition activity spans multiple countries: Australia, Germany, Canada, and France, where I competed in the Bocuse d'Or competition.

My passion lies in the culinary evolution most commonly known as molecular gastronomy (avant-garde cuisine).

Over the past six years I've been invited to present, demonstrate, and teach this modern cuisine to numerous culinary groups including GFTC, Humber College, and George Brown College.

My articles on the subject as well as other topics can be found frequently in Food and Hospitality Magazine as well as Food in Canada Magazine.

(Continued)

I recently set up John Placko Culinary Consulting (www.johnplacko.com) as a service to multi-unit restaurant companies and food manufacturers. I also launched Modern Culinary Academy (www.ModernCa.ca) to promote the awareness and education of molecular gastronomy.

My best dining experiences ever: El Bulli, Spain, and Noma, Denmark.
Photos of breakfast deconstructed and lemon meringue pies by John Placko.
Photo of John Placko by Shonah Chalmers CCC.

Types of Menus

Chapter 4

Most Common Types of Restaurant Menus

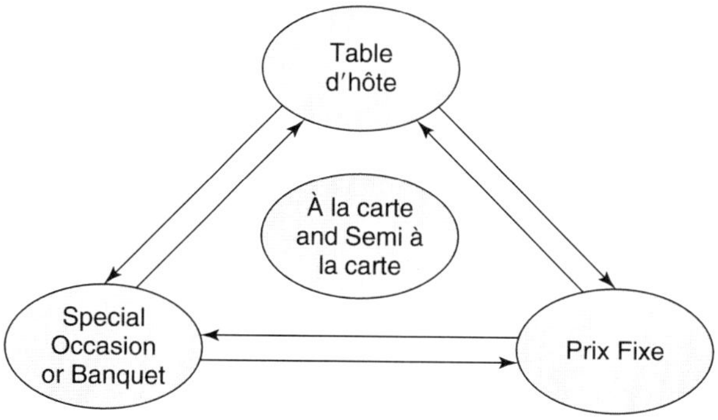

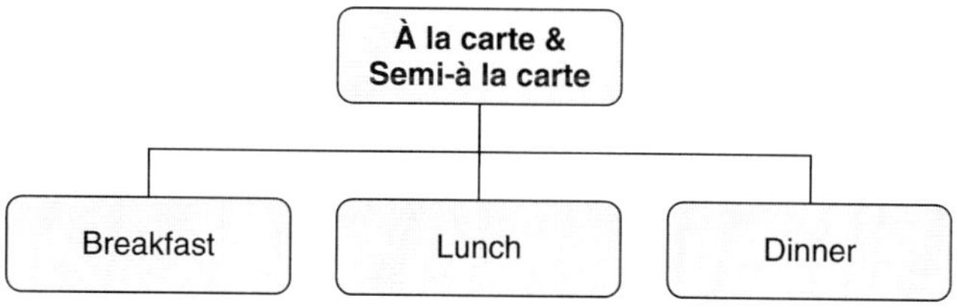

Menu Considerations

There are two basic types of menu concepts: **table d'hôte** and **à la carte - semi à la carte**. Table d'hôte implies several combined menu courses for one price while an à la carte menu has a separate price for each item. Menu writers often combine the two approaches by offering à la carte and set menu items, like specials, on one menu, or on a semi à la carte menu, main courses are often the main item paired with preset side dishes. There are advantages and disadvantages with both scenarios.

Other Types of Menus

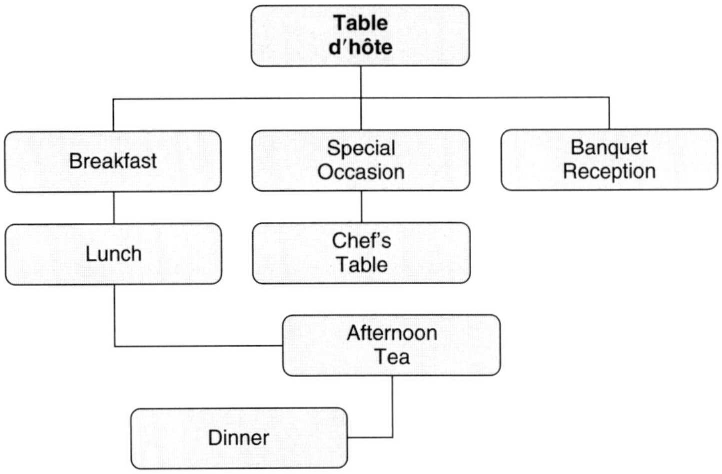

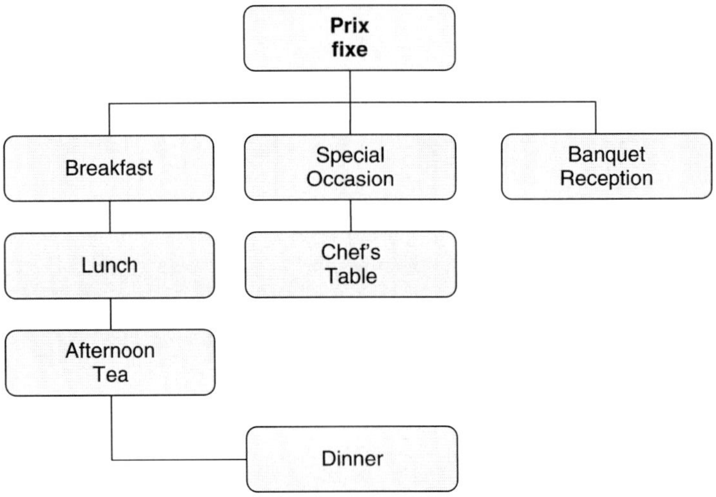

À la Carte Menu

Pronounced /a la kart/, the phrase was adopted into English in 1826.

Menu offerings based on each **meal period** (breakfast, lunch, and dinner) are listed in **customary eating sequence** (appetizers, soup, salads, main, desserts, and beverages) and all offerings are **priced individually**. Customers pay for each item they order.

When using this method, there is no need for exchange privileges. Customers have full control of what they select. As a menu planner, you assume no responsibility for their well-being. If a customer chooses to order three desserts and no appetizer or main course, it is his or her choice, healthy or not; whereas with table d'hôte or prix fixe menus, the chef has some responsibility to offer nutritionally balanced meals.

The menu may be one page or a whole booklet; it could be bound or inserted into a holder/cover—there is no rule how the physical menu is formatted. Traditionally, the actual menu has a formal, organized feel and look, using good quality white or creamy-coloured textured paper stock, script type characters, and black or blue ink. The quality of the paper stock and the overall appearance are usually in direct relation to the professed quality of the establishment.

Advantages of à la Carte Menus

Since every business depends on sales, when the opportunity arises to make a sale, maximising these sales should be a priority. This is normally achieved by verbally influencing customers to order the most profitable items on the menu and by recommending appetizers, soups, salads, side dishes, desserts, and appropriate wines with the meal (**up-selling**).

Due to the structure of an à la carte menu, when the customer orders side dishes, which are individually priced, to complement the main course, he or she knowingly or unknowingly builds up sales and cheque averages. Obviously, it is much easier to increase the cheque average when everything on the menu is priced individually. The server, by recommendations, will get the guests to order a separate vegetable, salad, beverage, appetizer, and so on. The total cheque may increase substantially often without full awareness of the customer. Example: The main item is priced at $25.00, and each side dish is $6.50. By the time the plate is assembled with three side dishes it will cost $44.50. If the same dish would have been offered on a semi à la carte menu, it most likely would have been packaged priced at $40.00. Four dollars and fifty cents of extra sales were achieved and the customer got exactly what he or she wanted without any wastage due to dislike and without any exchange privileges for items they may not be fond of.

As previously indicated, customers are in control (empowered), selecting and ordering exactly what they want, any item from the menu, in any order. If they do not want a soup, they do not order one; if they want only a salad, dessert, and coffee, that is what they order. Unless the customer was not aware of the actual cost, a win-win sale was concluded.

Potential Disadvantages of à la Carte Menus

Consumers may not realize, unless so told, that by ordering à la carte they can pick and choose as few or as many items as they desire and may perceive à la carte offerings as an attempt to increase prices in comparison with a semi à la carte menu where main course items usually include side dishes in their pricing. This can lead to an upsetting situation when customers now have to pay $2.00 for bread and butter, something that was formerly included with the meal.

To change menu item selling prices requires a great deal of information, recalculation of **standard recipes** to ensure fluctuation of ingredient costs are passed on to the consumer to ensure appropriate **profit margins**.

It is also considerably more difficult to forecast the results of repricing an à la carte menu than a table d'hôte menu, not only because of the consumer-made selection (**menu mix, sales mix, popularity index**) but also due to the many more items needed for an à la carte or semi à la carte menu compared to table d'hôte and prix fixe menus.

Most menus today, due to customer's feedback and demands offer a *combination of both concepts*. The advantages and disadvantages are the same as discussed above.

Semi à la Carte Menu

The semi à la carte menu resembles the structure of an à la carte menu; however, some of the individually priced menu items are combined (menu items served with accompaniments, side dishes, salad, etc.). This method may lead to customers requesting menu item substitutions or exchanges.

See example of a semi à la carte listed menu items on page 33.

California-Style Menu

Originating in California, similar in structure to the à la carte or semi à la carte menu, the California-style menu offers all available meal periods on one card, often using modern, non-formal fonts, coloured backgrounds, graphics, and even comical characters, creating or contributing to a relaxed, easy-going atmosphere.

The California style menu will most likely utilise a **tri-, four-** or **six-panel menu** layout in order to combine and organise the different meal types and periods.

A considerable amount of space is needed for the various sections, such as breakfast, lunch, afternoon tea, and dinner, and the required sub-sections for appetizers, soups, salads, mains, desserts, and beverages.

A menu, like a room-service menu offering items available at any time, is also considered to be a California-style menu. This style of menu is well-suited for cafés, bistros, brasseries, and pubs, for example.

Advantages of a California-Style Menu

For the customer: Items are all on one card; if properly sectioned, it is easy for the guest to navigate and to make a selection. For the operator: There is no need to have several different menus printed.

Potential Disadvantages of a California-Style Menu

Due to the great variety of products on one menu, product cost changes will require updating and reprinting the whole menu (all sections and pages) instead of the meal-period-ones only. Menus featuring four-or two-colour graphics and perhaps various font colours are rather expensive to print. Some customers may find menus with multiple pages difficult to hold and handle and too much to read at once, slowing them down in placing an order and subsequently delaying the service and occupying the available chair for quite some time, thereby reducing the table turnover rate.

Table d'hôte and Prix Fixe (and Today's Tasting Menus)

Table d'hôte directly translated into English literally means "host's table" or "the table of the host" In the 16th century, it originally referred to a table shared by guests, where a meal based on a set menu was served at a specific time. On restaurant menus, however, table d'hôte refers to a complete meal of several courses. Because the host's table menu was a set menu, the cutlery for the table setting was easily predetermined.

In the 19th century, the meaning shifted to include any meal featuring a complete (set) menu with a limited number of choices at a preset fixed price (prix fixe, which is pronounced in English like "prefix").

A prix fixe menu is a collection of predetermined menu items presented as a multi-course meal at a set price.

A restaurant may offer for lunch or dinner a prix fixe menu of smoked salmon appetizer, beef roulade for the main course, a cheese sampler plate for the third course, and Peach Melba as dessert.

There are no set rules for selecting menu items for a table d'hôte or prix fixe menu. Items are often selected from the regular menu in order to try out future specials.

Many Continental and European-style restaurants may actually offer two or more prix fixe options to their guests. A table d'hôte or prix fixe menu might be presented as a special of the day, printed separately from an à la carte menu, or it is promoted in an outdoor billboard, on a blackboard, or verbally by the server. Often the bundled table d'hôte or prix fixe menu offerings are less expensive than the same items selected from the à la carte menu. Chefs usually prepare in anticipation for needed quantities and once all are sold, these choices may no longer be available.

Table d'hôte or prix fixe menus should be printed on a single sheet of paper and presented separately from the standard menu. Like all menus, use of good quality paper and a font that is easy to read, even for the aging population, is very important. As mentioned before, the appearance and feel of the paper, the type and colour of the type-font may lead toward a perception of quality.

Include your restaurant's name at the top and contact information on the bottom of the menu. Some guests keep (collect) menus, especially if they liked the food, ambiance, and service, to show their friends and to help them to locate the establishment again. (To avoid the high cost of reprinting disappearing menus, offer customers the scaled-down version of the full menu). Each menu offering should have a brief description. If the menu offerings are in a foreign language, ensure that a proper translation and/or explanation is available. Avoid using clip art or drawings and photographs.

Although I have advised to avoid using clip art or drawings and photographs on the menu, it is becoming increasingly popular in metropolitan cities' restaurants to show photographs of menu items to assist foreign travellers who are not familiar with the native language to make an informed selection.

Advantages of Table d'hôte and Prix Fixe Menus

Selling price calculations and required changes are relatively simple since less information is required, and it is easier to attain. If there are twelve items (two soups, three appetizers, four main course items, and three desserts) on the menu, only twelve prices need to be calculated and balanced. An à la carte menu with twelve entrees and the separately offered soups, appetizers, salads, side dishes, and desserts may have thirty to fifty prices to consider.

Since item pricing is a very effective way to influence the sales mix, the balancing of forty to fifty prices is definitely more complex than twelve items.

With a classic table d'hôte or prix fixe menu, consumers can decide easily by selecting an entrée; all other selection decisions have been made for them. Although it is common to have choices of the side dishes or main course exchange privileges, it is still easier for the consumer to make selections from a classic table d'hôte or prix fixe menu than from an à la carte menu.

This in turn could increase seat turnover since guests will need less time to make a decision because the selection is limited and the menu items have already been prepped.

Potential Disadvantages of Table d'hôte and Prix Fixe Menus

Pricing is inflexible. Pricing is easier since it is less complex, but you lose some of the ability to influence selection decisions with reduced price combinations.

Wasted food can also be a problem. People get food they may not necessarily want, and it eventually is thrown away.

Guests may feel their meal costs too much. This concern is related to the above point. If they get food they do not want and do not eat, they may feel exploited because they had to pay for it. The price/value perception is negative.

You have fewer options for increasing check averages, which is in contrast to the primary advantage of the à la carte menu.

Degustation Menus (Type or Form of Tasting menu)

Degustation is from the French term *dégustation* and is commonly used in the English language to describe an "attentive, appreciative tasting of a variety of selected foods" most often prepared from exquisite or specialty food items, intended to stimulate and challenge the senses and the gustatory system. Traditionally presented as an eight-course menu, consisting of "teaser portions," small samplings, paired with appropriate wines or selected imported beers.

Limited Menu

The term refers to a menu that is limited in its offerings. This term would apply to all previously mentioned menu types that have fewer items to select from than the standard menus of the same type. A legitimate question would be, What is the standard? There are no set rules. If your menu offers fewer choices than the direct competition (same type of establishment), then your menu, in comparison, is limited.

Cycle, Cyclical Menus, and Meal Plans

(See sample in the following pages)

Are sets of menus for meal periods repeating on specific days, weeks, or over a set time period? This type of menu is mainly used in institutions such as hospitals, children's or sports camps, cruise ships, and resorts where guests are expected to stay for one or multiple weeks, or in a penitentiary or a long-term care facility where occupants stay for a longer period of time, as well as airlines and trains where most travellers take a round trip and then do not travel the same route for some time again, if at all.

A cruise ship offering a two-week cruise will repeat the two-week cycle menu at the beginning of each cruise. Other institutions, like a hospital or long-term care facility may use a six-week cycle. Since this cycle would include weekends and maybe some holidays, it is advisable to have some special meals for the weekend and holidays to break the routine.

Advantages of Cyclical Menus

These plans are easy to purchase for, to control, and to prepare for, since the quantity and type of products do not vary very much from cycle to cycle.

Potential Disadvantages of Cyclical Menus

Since the host assumes responsibility for the well-being of the guests under his or her care during the length of their stay, and sometimes beyond, it is the host's legal responsibility to ensure that the meals are nutritionally well balanced and healthy.

In most cases, hospitals, prisons, and long-term care facilities engage nutritionists to ensure that the meals are well balanced.

In the above mentioned example of the cruise ship, instead of preparing a **meal plan** for the duration of the trip, a buffet is offered for each meal period so that the guests can make their own decisions and thus assume responsibility for their own wel- being.

TABLE 1 Alphabetical Summary Common Types of Menus

à la carte	All offered menu items are priced separately
semi à la carte	Like à la carte, however, main course offerings usually are paired with side dishes.
California	All meal period offerings are on one card. Casual, colourful appearance.
cycle/cyclical/institutional/meal plan	Repeats offerings after a set period of timed intervals.
dégustation	Set menu, set selling price
dietary, spa, and/or nutritional	To satisfy dietary or nutritional needs, like sodium and/or cholesterol reduced . . .
du jour	Menu of the day, should change daily
hybrid	A combination of static or cycle and market menu
market	Usually for shorter periods of time utilizing seasonal market items. Carbon print and 100 miles rules compliant.
prix fixe	A selection of combined offerings of listed courses for the same fixed or set selling price
set menu for special occasion or banquet	Limited menu offerings for social or business functions
static	A menu, or a section of a menu that does not change. Commonly used in speciality and ethnic restaurants.
table d'hôte	Different selections of combined offerings of listed courses may have a different selling price.
other	This may include fad menus such as acid and alkaline balanced menus.

Of course, guests must have healthy and nutritious products available; staff should be able to offer guidance to the inexperienced.

Menu Formats

The **French classical menu** is a sixteen-course menu comprised of hors d'oeuvres (appetizer), potage (soup), oeufs (eggs), farineaux (rice and pasta), poisson (fish), entrée (entry of first meat course), sorbet (flavoured water), reléve (meat course), rôti (roast), légumes (vegetables), salades (salad), buffet froid (cold buffet), entremet de sûcre (sweets), savoureaux (savoury), fromage (cheese), desserts (fresh fruits and nuts), and cafe (coffee). In our multicultural society, today's menus are often mixed and blended to meet the various needs and demands of customers.

The Classical Banquet Menu Format

Eight-Course Dinner Menu

Appetizer	Les Hors d'Oeuvres Variés
Soup	Potage
Fish Entrée	Poisson
Sherbet	Sorbet
Poultry or Meat Main Course	Plat de Résistance
(Vegetables & Starch)	(Légumes)
Salad	Salade
Cheeses	Fromages
Dessert	Dessert
Coffee-Tea	Café-Thé

The Contemporary Banquet Menu Format

BREAKFAST	LUNCH	DINNER
Juices	Soup	Soup or Salad (hot/cold)
Fruits	Salad	Salad or Soup (cold/hot)
Cereals	Main course ~ Entrée	Fish dish
Eggs & Omelettes	(Vegetables and Starch)	Main course ~ Entrée
Fish or Meat	Dessert	(Vegetables and Starch)
(Vegetables and Starch)	Coffee-Tea	Dessert
Pancakes and alike		Coffee-Tea
Breads ~ Quick breads		Please note:
Coffee-Tea		Sorbet/Sherbet was left out purposely.

TABLE 2 Menu Occasion Types: Breakfast (B), Lunch (L), Dinner (D)

ALPHABETICALLY	BY TIME OF THE DAY, FROM AM TO PM
Afternoon meals	Breakfast (B)
Banquet/Reception	Brunch
Beverage/Cocktails	Luncheon (L)
Breakfast	Afternoon meals
Brunch	Low tea
Catering	Dinner/Pre-theatre (D)
Chef's table	High Tea (D)
Children	Formal Dinner (D)
Coffee break	Chef's table (L/D)
Dinner/Pre-theatre	Late evening—after theatre
High Tea	Today's specials—du jour (usual B/L/D)
Institutional/Food Services	
In-Room dining	
Late evening	
Low tea	
Luncheon	
Take out	
Today's specials—du jour	

TABLE 3 Common Meal Period and Menu Usage

	Type of Menu			
MEAL PERIOD	À LA CARTE OR SEMI À LA CARTE	CALIFORNIA	BANQUET OR SET MENU	TABLE D'HÔTE OR PRIX FIXE
Breakfast	X	X	X	X
Brunch	X		X	X
Luncheon	X	X	X	X
Afternoon meals	X		X	X
High Tea			X	
Low Tea	X		X	X
Dinner	X	X	X	X
Formal Dinner	X		X	X
Late evening	X		X	X
Breaks	X		X	X

Sample Menus

Six-Day Sample Menu

Six-Day Sample Menu—Locate page 1 (left page) opposite to page 2

	SIX DAY MENU		ALL MEALS ARE
	DAY ONE	DAY TWO	DAY THREE
BREAKFAST			
	CARROT AND APPLE JUICE	FRESHLY SQUEEZED ORANGE JUICE	ORGANIC GRAPEFRUIT JUICE
	HOT OATMEAL WITH HONEY AND CINNAMON	EGGS FLORENTINE WITH SAUCE CHORON	GRILLED WILD BOAR SAUSAGE GARNISHED WITH SUNDRIED BLUEBERRIES
	MORNING GLORY MUFFINS W/ A SIDE SERVING OF MACADAMIA BUTTER	BRAISED ARTICHOKE HEARTS STUFFED WITH CHESTNUT PASTE	BROILED TOMATO SPRINKLED WITH BASIL OLIVE OIL, PARMESAN SODA BREAD
LUNCH			
SOUP OR APPETIZER	FENNEL PISTACHIO SOUP WITH MAPLE WHIPPED CREAM ROSETTE	ARCTIC CHAR TERRINE WITH SCALLOP CENTER -MARKED WITH TRIO OF PEPPER COULIS	MARINATED PERCH, SHRIMP, AND SCALLOP KABOBS WITH A PEAR MARMALADE
MAIN	6 OZ GUINEA HEN BREAST STUFFED WITH DATES AND PASSION FRUIT ON 4 OZ LEMON PEPPERED LINGUINE TOSSED WITH SNOW PEAS AND JULIENNE CARROTS STEEPED IN BRANDY	6 OZ PORK FILET MEDALLIONS 3 OZ SWEET POTATO & ROSEMARY DUCHESSE AVOCADO MOUSSE COATED WITH BLACK CURRENT PRESERVE	5 OZ ORANGE PEPPERS STUFFED WITH COUSCOUS AND ZUCCHINI 3 OZ WILD RICE WITH BUTTON MUSHROOMS 3 OZ SAUTÉED SWISS CHARD WITH PINE NUTS AND LEMON ZEST
DESSERT	HONEYDEW AND CANTALOUPE WITH MINTED SYRUP	BAKED BANANA DREAM WITH CITRUS AND CINNAMON TOPPED WITH CRÈME FRAICHE	BROWNIE BOMBE
DINNER			
SOUP OR APPETIZER	BUFFALO CARPACCIO DRAPED OVER MARINATED RED LENTILS DRIZZLED WITH THYME OLIVE OIL	LOBSTER CONSOMMÉ GARNISHED WITH MUSSELS, JULIENNE CREPES AND ORANGE ZEST	CANARY MELON AND HAVARTI CHEESE IN PUFF PASTRY BUNDLES
MAIN	6 0Z FILLET OF SALMON W/ DUXELLES WRAPPED IN ROMAINE LEAVES IN A LIGHT KIWI CREAM SAUCE	6OZ DUCK BREAST STUFFED WITH VEAL SWEETBREADS AND GORGONZOLA CHEESE	2 TO 3 OZ GRILLED QUAIL WRAPPED IN PROSCIUTTO STUFFED WITH FIGS AND PORCINI MUSHROOMS
SIDE	RAPINI RISOTTO WITH PEACH SEGMENTS	POMMES ANNA BASE GARNISHED WITH PAPAYA & MANGO CHUTNEY	CELERY WITH BASIL BRAISED IN CHICKEN STOCK
SIDE	RED CABBAGE WITH APPLE AND RAISINS BRAISED IN WINE	BROCCOLI AND CAULIFLOWER TOSSED IN HAZELNUT BUTTER	PECAN RICE WITH FENNEL AND PEARL ONIONS
SALAD	GRILLED EGGPLANT AND BELGIUM ENDIVE SPRINKLED WITH ROASTED WALNUTS AND SUNDRIED TOMATO VINAIGRETTE	MESCLUN SALAD WITH POPPY SEED VINAIGRETTE	WATERCRESS ALFALFA SPROUTS WITH RED WINE VINAIGRETTE
DESSERT	STRAWBERRY SHORTCAKE WITH CRÈME ANGLAISE	PINEAPPLE PARFAIT	CRÊPE SIMON FRANGIPANE AND CHERRY JAM

Six-Day Sample Menu—Page two

	ACCOMPANIED	BY A SELECTION	OF BEVERAGES
	DAY FOUR	DAY FIVE	DAY SIX
BREAKFAST			
	FRESH GRAPE JUICE	HONEYED STRAWBERRY SORBET GARNISHED WITH MINT AND MISTED WITH CHAMPAGNE	TOMATO JUICE WITH CHIFFONADE OF CELERY LEAVES
	POACHED PEAR DRAPED WITH BING CHERRIES SERVED OVER BELGIUM WAFFLES, FLAMBÉED WITH GRAND MARNIER AT THE TABLE		SWISS MUESLI WITH GARDEN FRESH DICED APPLES AND PEACHES
		LEMON RICOTTA PANCAKES WITH A LEMON SYRUP GARNISHED W/ BACON WRAPPED PRUNES	STRAWBERRIES AND GRAPES W/ BRIE KABOBS
LUNCH			
SOUP OR APPETIZER	CHILLED VODKA WATER MELON SOUP GARNISHED WITH HONEYDEW AND CHIVES	PARSNIP PURÉE SOUP WITH HEARTS OF PALM AND CHIVE GARNISH	FIDDLEHEAD SOUP GARNISHED WITH PIMENTO
MAIN	6 OZ SHARK STEAK WITH GRILLED PINEAPPLE ON COCONUT CREAM TOPPED WITH CUCUMBER MOON SALAD 4 OZ QUINOA PILAF W/ STAR FRUIT 4 OZ JERUSALEM ARTICHOKE SOUFFLÉ	5 OZ SAUTÉED GARLIC SHRIMP ON 4 OZ MARINATED SPAGHETTI SQUASH 3 OZ BASMATI RRICE SAUTÉED W/ GREEN ONION AND PEAS	6 OZ OSTRICH GALANTINE WITH JUS GARNISHED WITH LEMON ZEST 3 OZ BARLEY RISOTTO W/ SHIITAKE MUSHROOMS AND SPINACH 3 OZ PECAN CARROTS
DESSERT	GINGER ICE CREAM WITH CANDIED CHOCOLATE ORANGE PEEL	STEWED APRICOTS SERVED ON COCONUT MERINGUE	CHOCOLATE MOUSSE WITH ALMOND SHORTCAKE
DINNER			
SOUP OR APPETIZER	PAN FRIED SOFT SHELL CRAB HALF WRAPPED IN PHYLLO PASTRY DRAPED WITH RATATOUILLE	CLAM AND CHEESE STUFFED CELERY SERVED WITH SPINACH CHÈVRE PHYLLO TRIANGLES	EGGPLANT AND OLIVE ANTIPASTO ON RADICCHIO
MAIN	6 OZ ROASTED ROSEMARY GARLIC CHICKEN BREAST STUFFED WITH CASHEWS AND BUFFALO MOZZARELLA	8 OZ SAFFRON PASTA W/ THYME SCENTED CELERY BROTH	MARINATED IN A TARRAGON POMMERY DIJON MUSTARD ROASTED 10 OZ RACK OF LAMB BLACK BEAN SALAD BRAISED IN BRANDY, LINED WITH BLUEBERRY CRÈME FRAICHE SHIITAKE AND PORTABELLA MUSHROOM STRUDEL
SIDE	BEETS IN ORANGE REDUCTION	ASPARAGUS SPEARS MARINATED IN WHITE WINE VINEGAR	
SIDE	SAUTÉED GREEN BEANS IN TARRAGON VINAIGRETTE	ROASTED CORN WITH ZUCCHINI	
SALAD	MARINATED TOMATO WITH BOCCONCINI CHEESE SERVED ON ROMAINE LETTUCE	MOULDED CRANBERRY & GRAPE MOUSSE SALAD	HEARTS OF ESCAROLE WITH KUMQUAT AND PEAR MARMALADE
DESSERT	GREENAGE PLUMS IN PORT	CARAMEL BREAD PUDDING	CRÈME BRÛLÉE W/ BING CHERRIES

High Tea versus Low Tea

During the well-known **afternoon tea**, service includes scones and crumpets with Devonshire cream, jams and marmalades, finger or tea sandwiches, and of course dainty pastries and a variety of teas. This is referred to as **low tea**, the reason being that it is usually presented and served on a **low table** in a sitting room, a parlour, or in a reception area. Afternoon tea is most often served between lunch and dinner, or from 2:30 p.m. to 5:00 p.m.

The **high tea**, which actually represents an early dinner, was served in the late afternoon to hard-working labourers who did not have an opportunity for breaks or to eat lunch on a high table. **High tea** often consisted of meat pies, Welsh rarebit, kippers, steak and kidney pie. The offerings changed with location between Wales, Scotland, Ireland, and England.

Children's Menu

Children love to have their own menu featuring their favourite food items, yet their food is usually decided by the parent(s). Parents are often pressured by their offspring's desire to bring them where they can have that "special meal (and the toys) as seen on TV." They like intriguing, colourful menus and, depending on their age, are looking for characters they can recognize. Many restaurants that cater to smaller children have placemats with themes and activities printed especially for them.

Not all restaurants want to attract kids, but if parents bring them along, they would be looking for either a separate children's menu or a section on the menu identifying dishes suitable for children, usually smaller in size and priced lower than adult meals. To qualify for the children's menu items there often is an age limit.

Restaurants, in their efforts to avoid having separate listings for children, often simply list two sizes, such as small or large portions for some or all menu items. Theoretically, this is potentially misleading and subsequently should not be offered. See the "Menu Law Section" on page 71.

From "The Onion", America's Finest News Source

www.theonion.com/content/node/39384

WASHINGTON, DC—Historians and scholars nationwide heralded the discovery of a children's menu on the back of one of the four original charters of the U.S. Constitution, said Archivist of the United States, John Carlin.

U.S. Constitution and the And Children's Menu, originally drawn up at the Constitutional Convention in Philadelphia in 1787, is housed at the National Archives Building.

The menu—on the back of Article I, which establishes a bicameral Congress comprising the Senate and the House of Representatives—provides dining options for children under 7.

"In this discovery, we see yet another example of the wisdom of our founding fathers," Carlin said. "While establishing a government that honours both the rights of the individuals and the unity of the

nation, they also recognized the need for fun-to-eat, affordable dining options for the nation's youngest Americans."

Until now, scholars had focused on the elegant calligraphy on the Constitution's front, entirely overlooking the reverse side, which features two columns of fancifully named menu items, such as Yankee Doodle Macaroni, Jumping Johnnycakes, and Eagle Fingers.

"The wording of the Constitution is general, necessitating interpretation, and the same can be said for its children's menu," Carlin said. "We do not know exactly what the framers of the Constitution meant by 'Eagle Fingers.'"

Strict constructionists are likely to assume that they were strips of eagle flesh fried in batter, but loose constructionists might argue that the term was an amusing way to encourage children to eat their chicken or grouse.

Other dishes found by researchers include Bloody Great Blood Pudding, Cheese Betwixt two Slices of Bread, and Mother Goose.

The menu is offered "for children of weaning age until seven years."

"The menu reflects the relative brevity of childhood more than two centuries ago," Carlin said. "Contemporary children's menus are generally offered to children of up to 12 years of age."

Near the bottom of the document, a waxy, bluish spot almost obscures a line drawing of a man with a peg-leg.

"We believe the caricature could be Gouverneur Morris of Pennsylvania, who wore a wooden leg—but it might just be a pirate," Carlin said.

"Whatever it is, its strong proof that the 'Pleasant Diversions' section of the menu was used by a child, as the figure had been coloured in rather inexpertly, in blue from head-to-foot."

Near the stain is a small maze leading statesman and Constitution-signer Benjamin Franklin to a lightning-struck kite. To the right of this is the earliest-known example of a word-find, containing the names of Revolutionary War-era battleships.

So far, no adult menu has been found.

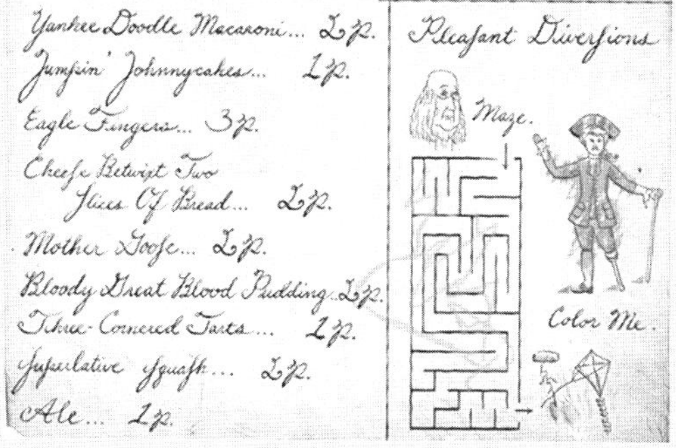

Menu Layout Samples

One page (front & back)
No cover or page holder

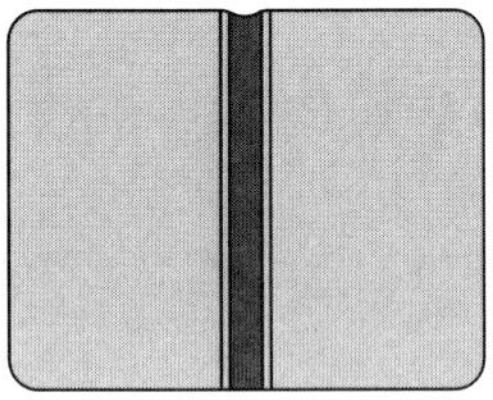

Two pages (most common style) Outside cover, front & back, two inside panels/pages. Bound or sleeves.

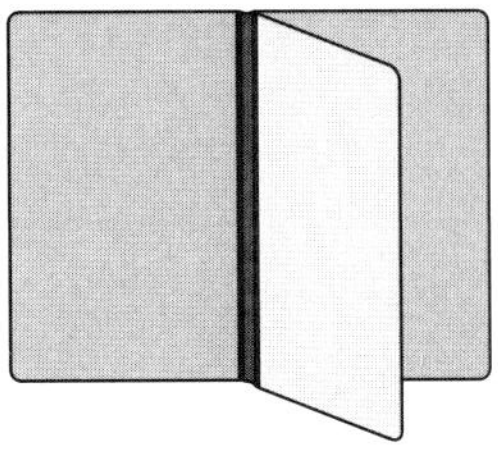

Tri-panel, four pages Outside cover, front & back, three inside panels can be used for food & beverage offerings as well as for the **Institutional Copy**. Bound or sleeves.

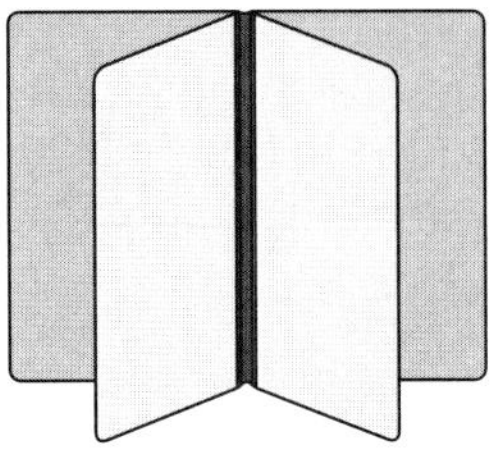

Four-panel, six page menu Outside cover, front & back, Inside pages can be used for food and beverage offerings as well as for the institutional copy. Bound or sleeves.

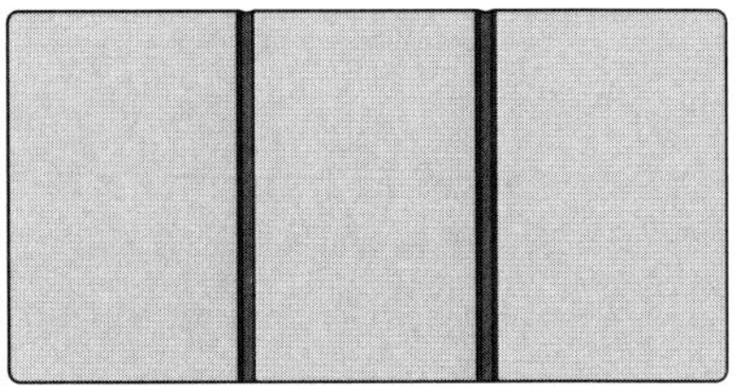

Tri-panel folding, Outside cover, front back and middle. Inside pages can be used for food and beverage offerings as well as for the institutional copy. Bound or sleeves.

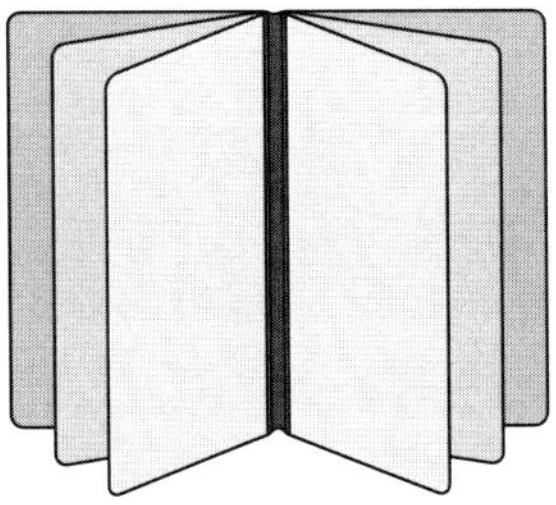

Six panels, ten pages,
Bound or sleeves.

Hard-cover outside with printed page insert, one panel/page can be used for daily, à la carte or set menu.

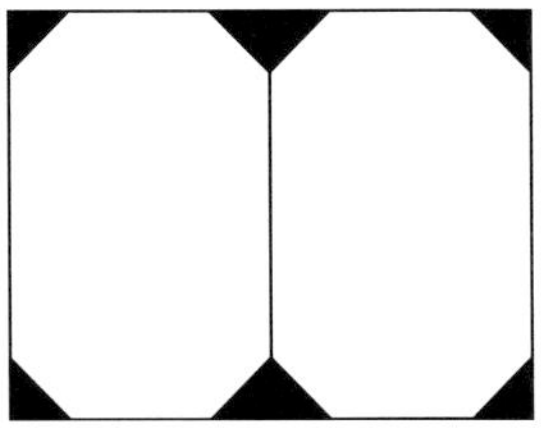

Hard-cover outside with two inserts for printed pages. Two panel/pages. Can be used with one fixed à la carte page, one daily hanging page, and/or for specialty menu items.

Menu board—can be used outdoors or indoors

Special occasion menu

Font Styles

Fonts used on a menu should communicate the type, style and atmosphere of an establishment and address the reader's mood.

All font styles are displayed in **16 point size** (this one is Calibri Body).

Literally thousands of fonts have been created over the years, with new ones emerging daily from which to choose. Word-processing software includes many types of free fonts, such as TT True type, MT Monotype, or PostScript fonts. Microsoft Office includes approximately 500 fonts, and many more can be obtained (purchased or free of charge) from various web-pages (**www.1001freefonts.com**).

For illustrated font, font colour and paper colour, and font colours on different paper backgrounds, please visit www.menuforprofit.com—Menu section.

TABLE 4 Example Font Styles and Usage

ELEGANT, TRADITIONAL, FOR FESTIVE OCCASIONS	FOR EVERY DAY WRITING—NO LEGS "SANS SERIF"	FOR EVERY DAY WRITING—WITH LEGS "SERIF"	FOR DIFFERENT APPLICATIONS
Edwardian Script ITC	Verdena	Bookman Old Style	Australian Sunrise
Pristina	AvantGarde	Times News Roman	Bauhaus 93
Freestyle Script	Helvetica	Book Antiqua	Chiller
French Script MT	Arial	Century	Gigi
Vladimir Script	Antique Olive Roman	Cambria	Alba Super
Old English Text MT	Franklin Gothic Book	Perpetua	Lucida Handwriting
Lucida Calligraphy	Tahoma	Occidental	Broadway

Other Menu Formats

Printed menu
Verbal menu
Digital: menu boards, web pages
Digital streamed menus
Menu boards (easels, chalkboards)
LED panels
Projected menus
Placemat menus
Menus in place holders

The Next Step: Managing the Menu

Illustrated is a sample semi à la carte menu, based on the types of menus featuring these offerings.

CATEGORY/GROUPS	ITEM	HOT	COLD	TOTAL
Appetizers, Soups, and Salads	Appetizers	3	2	5
	Soups	2	1	3
	Salads	1 warm	3	4
	Rice dishes	1		1
	Breads	2 warm		2
Entrées	Pasta dishes	2		2
	Rice dishes	2		2
	Beef	3		3
	Veal	2		2
	Pork	1		1
	Offals—Innards	1		1
	Poultry	3		3
	Fish	2		2
	Crustaceans	1		1
	Mollusks	1		1
	Cephalopods	1		1
	Game/Game poultry	1		1
	Vegetarian/Vegan	1		1
	Healthy alternative	1		1
Side Dishes and Breads	Starch and Vegetable	6		6
	Specialty Breads	2 warm		2

CATEGORY/GROUPS	ITEM	HOT	COLD	TOTAL
Desserts	Ice creams/Sorbets		2	2
	Pies	1 warm		1
	Soufflés	1	or 1	1
	Tortes		2	2
	Healthy alternative	1	or 1	1
Cheeses	Selection		2	2
Coffee	With alcohol	2		2
	Plain	1		1
	Espresso/Cappuccino	2		2
Teas	Hot/Cold/Iced	Selection	1	10

Total Appetizers, Soups, and Salads: **15** Total Entrées: **22**

Total Desserts and Cheeses: **9** Total Breads and Side Dishes: **8**

Not including beverages, this menu features a total of forty-six items plus eight side dishes with a prep-list of approximately eighty to ninety ingredients including marinades, sauces, pasta doughs, and various vegetables and fruits.

One very important point in menu planning is **cross-utilization**, the utilization of each purchased product in a variety of applications.

This obviously is very simple with salt and flour, since it is used in a multitude of recipes, but it can become more challenging with other ingredients:

Shrimp: cocktails, hot dishes, open-faced sandwiches
Lobster: boiled, grilled, and cold dishes
Crabmeat: cold appetizer and hot dishes
Beef strip loin: as a steak or as an à la minute goulash (stroganoff)
Lettuce: salads and chiffonade
Tomatoes: salads and grilled tomatoes or tomato sauce
(Offal-Innards-Abates)Variety meats: for hot dishes or cold pâtés
Mollusks: raw or as hot dishes
Pasta: hot dishes or salads

It is a worthwhile exercise to prepare a cross-utilization list for **perishable products**, to be known as such and closely monitored/inventoried. If the fresh shrimp that were purchased for the shrimp cocktail don't sell as well as anticipated, perhaps they should be offered as a **special of the day** in a pasta dish, skewered and grilled, or in a dill sauce; as long as they are not lost and cause an increase to food cost.

Once the menu draft has been selected by the management team, the remaining food handling staff, cooks, and servers should have the opportunity to offer input. They should also be given an opportunity to create items based on their experience or on feedback from customers.

The opportunity to provide ideas, perhaps in conjunction with a contest, will demonstrate their importance to the business and usually increase moral.

The next step is to allocate all this information on a menu itself.

On pages 38 and 39 a small selection of available physical menu shapes/formats are illustrated. Selecting the two-panel menu for this example gives four pages, two outside and two inside.

Technically, the whole menu is referred to as the **menu copy**.

The outside areas (panels) are usually used for, but not limited to, the name of the establishment, a suitable graphic for the type and theme of the establishment, a welcoming or mission statement often including some historical information or perhaps featuring the owner or the chef, and other advertising and additional information, such as opening hours, contact and reservation information, or the physical address. The technical name for this copy: **institutional copy.** Important note: The institutional copy is not limited to the outside pages.

The two inside pages (panels) are used for merchandising the menu offerings and its technical name is **merchandising area**, which contains the **descriptive copy**.

The merchandising area—descriptive copy—features the food or beverage offerings based on headings that are organized in several sections, such as

Appetizers: hot or cold
Soups: hot or cold, cream, puree, or clear
Salads
Entrees: can also be subdivided into groups like; Beef, Pork, Veal, Poultry, Pasta, Seafood
Beverages, Alcoholic and Non-alcoholic
Add-ons and Clip-ons
Daily Specials and Prix fixe features
Cheese selection and desserts
Beverages: cold and hot are sometimes on a separate menu

The inside panels usually are able to hold two legal-sized (8½" x 14" or 18.75 CM x 30.9 CM) pages, a simple and effective way of communicating the various choices.

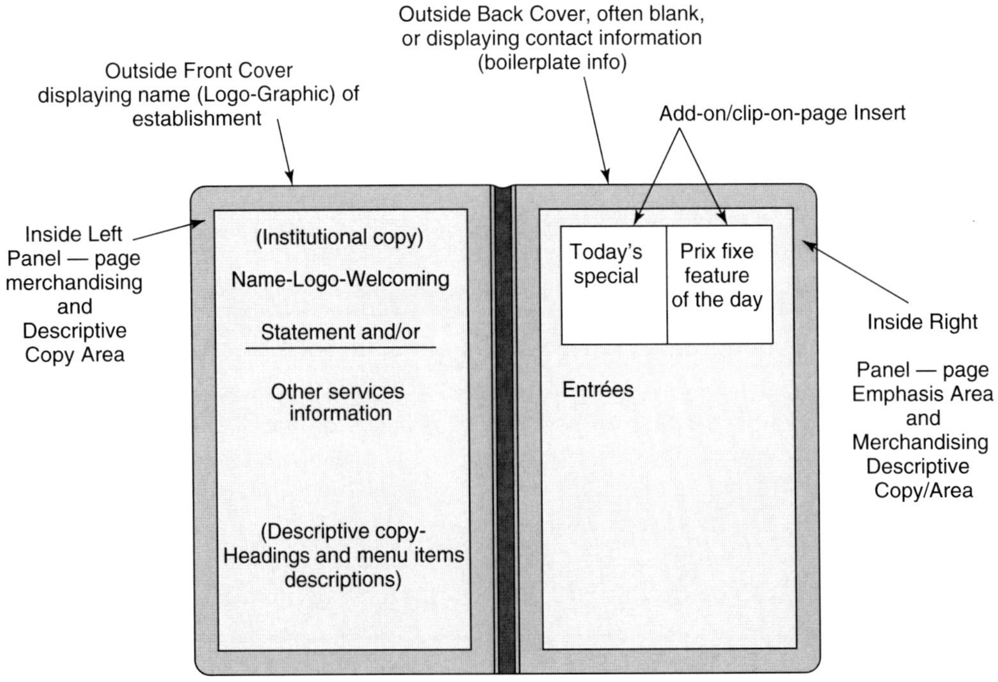

If there are more offerings than the pages can hold easily, additional pages should be added to avoid crowding of information.

Ideally, everything can be overseen on each page. Either on the front cover or on the left inside panel the institutional copy (welcoming statement) and any advertising or other available services, such as special functions, caterings etc. should be placed The actual menu headings and special offerings with items are listed in the descriptive copy area, in the order of traditional consumption.

The listing of menu items on the main menu traditionally include pastries, cheeses, and hot beverages, or these items are printed on a separate menu, making more room for entrées on the main menu. Listing "ending of a meal" items on a separate menu allows the customer time to revisit listed main menu items and to leisurely make a selection.

Quite often this separate menu features desserts, cheeses, cordials, cognacs, eaux de vie, specialty coffees and teas, providing a great opportunity to up-sell.

Apéritifs, cocktails, digestives, wine, and beer and other beverage offerings can be on a third panel/page or on a separate menu. A separate menu is often more practical since it is customary to have the guest select a drink or wine prior to the meal, as well as during the meal, so the guests can make a different wine selection to match each course.

Add-ons

Please note that the featured menu on page 42 shows an "add-on-insert" located on the top of the right the page to promote the special of the day or the prix fixe or table d'hôte menu.

Several studies have been made as to where the eye focuses onto the menu, referred to as **emphasis area**. The results of these studies seem to be somewhat different from each other and/or contradicting themselves. Since a menu is not read like a book—each page from the left top to the bottom of the page—a person looking at a menu, after absorbing the makeup and layout, will focus on the first unusual—text in bold or framed, a graphic or a picture, and on anything other than the standard text.

This area for an add-on may not exist if the establishment does not offer any specials or packages or if the advertised specials are posted on a menu-board, or printed on a separate menu card or communicated by the server.

An add-on is a fixed-size piece of paper to be inserted or clipped onto a designated area on the menu.

There are two common and one rarely used add-ons:

1. Inserted into a precut window or windows.
2. Inserted into a cellophane or plastic see-through sleeve.
3. Clipped onto the designated area using a small plastic clip. These clips were often provided by companies in various colors advertising their name: green clips with the name Perrier in white on it, yellow or red clips with the name of Heinz in white, etc.

The clip-on at its inception was very popular until operators realized that stacking menus became a problem since the plastic clip that was glued on the menu created a small bulge and the folded menus did not lay down flat anymore. Also, the clips eventually rubbed against the opposite page wearing the print and/or the sleeve.

Advantages of Using Add-ons

Add-ons are easy to change and exchange.Once the featured product is sold out, the add-on is simply removed or replaced with another add-on featuring another item.

Disadvantages of Using Add-ons

If there is no other special item(s) to be featured, it leaves a peculiar blank space on the menu.

And How Do Most Readers of Menus React to Your Menu Layout?

There have been studies on how people read a menu with contradicting results. No scientific proof has been established if people read menus from the top left to the right bottom, from left to right, or as some suggest, from the bottom up. I firmly believe that someone who looks at an à la carte menu, regardless if it is a single page or multiple pages, the first thing he or she will notice is something outstanding, like capitalized or bolded text, a change in font size or type, captions, clip or add-ons, graphics, and different colours.

Most consumers will be looking at headings to locate what they came to eat: appetizers, soups, salads, main courses, and their subgroups like types of appetizers, soups, salads, and main courses, such as meats, seafood or pasta, vegetarian or vegan dishes. Once the offerings are located, a more detailed reading of the offerings will take place. At this point it will be the item's ingredients, composition, seasoning, and cooking methods, and in some cases the cost, that will sell the consumer. This is where the menu writer needs to be using words that clearly differentiate the individual item from other offerings, to attract and encourage consumers to order. Emphasis should be on the most profitable items. The palatable description of the emphasized item must make that difference.

Dessert menus are often listed on a separate menu, if not on the à la carte menu, and may be combined with complimenting beverages. These menus should be brought to the table after the main course has been consumed.

Menu Copy

Chapter 5

"Menu copy" is the term used for describing the physical menu, as compared to the area on the menu listing the offerings, which is referred to as "descriptive copy."

The menu should be written to appeal to all of the five senses. Actually, there are six, if you include Umami, which describes savouriness.

One eats with more than the mouth and the stomach, and it is important to remember and recognize this fact. Excite the eye and please the palate.

The food preparation, including presentation, must follow through with the written promises/commitments.

Sight: Describe the contrast of colours and shapes.
(Including prominent garnishes)
Taste: Explain prominent flavour and the methods of preparation.
Touch/Bite: Describe the various consistencies of the food.
Smell: Hint at the aroma of what is to come.
Hearing: Sell the sizzle.

Basic Rules

The following points are to be strongly considered when writing a menu.

A customer will relate and compare (mentally) the description to the finished product.

1. **COLOUR:** Products used on each plate should have:
   - No inappropriate duplication of colour
   - Individual items prepared to their gastronomically correct colour
2. **TEXTURE:** The texture of each individual item must be to the following standards:
   - No unnecessary duplication of texture on each plate
   - Each individual item prepared to the identified degree of "doneness"
   - Each individual item is cooked to the gastronomically correct, uniform textural consistency
3. **PORTION SIZE:** Each individual item must be to the described portion as identified on the menu.
4. **BALANCE:** The compatibility of shape and proportion of items on each plate presentation.

5. **PLATE PRESENTATION (including garnishes):** All presentations to be displayed to their menu/recipe description, optimizing visual appeal and arranged for ease of customers' handling with the available eating utensils.
   - **Garnishes:** Most dishes do not need a garnish. The presentation of the key/main item should be built from one or all ingredient, so as not to require additional items.
   - Garnishes should always be edible.
   - Ensure that the flavour of the garnish will not interfere with the flavour of the key/main item.
   - The size of the garnish should complement the key/main item and not draw attention away from it.
   - Garnishes, ideally should not be raw, and should be part of the main item served, i.e., pan-fried filet of a fish garnished with a shaped, crisp skin of the same fish.

6. **TASTE:** As defined by the menu description.
   - Complementing flavours of each presentation, i.e., no overpowering individual flavour. Seasoning must enhance the natural flavour.
   - Seasoning—as defined by recipe reference.
   - Seasoning may escalate from the start of the meal to the last course consumed, excluding desserts. When the palate is confronted with a strong seasoning at first it may not be able to taste milder seasoning afterwards.

7. **COOKING—PREP METHOD:** As defined by the menu description and recipe.
   - Pre-preparation methods such as marinating, pickling, curing, and smoking, as well as cooking method must be appropriate for the product being used and/or in accordance with classical method if the menu item bears a classical name.
   - All pre-preparation and cooking methods must be mentioned by the menu item's description.

Besides the five senses, there are psychological factors to be considered, such as moods and feelings. Someone who is in a good mood and feels well will most likely look at everything in a positive way and be somewhat forgiving, whereas someone in a bad frame of mind will most likely look at everything that does not please them in a negative way and may actually look for faults.

Knowing this, everyone in sales or customer service must aim to have customers in a positive frame of mind.

There are simple things we can do to affect the mood and feelings:

- Give the welcome feeling. Greeting customers with respect and a friendly smile and asking what can be done for them is the first step toward a positive impression.
- Everybody likes to be pampered without being treated condescendingly.
- If it is a repeat customer, knowing and greeting him or her with a first or last name will make him or her feel important. Thanking them for their repeat business will make them feel appreciated.
- Being attentive throughout the service, making recommendations, and ensuring that all is served as ordered, inquiring about the satisfaction with their products ordered, not only demonstrate that you care; it most likely will earn the appropriate tip.

How Do We (mind and body) Experience the Taste of Food?

Flavour equals **taste**, plus **mouthfeel**, plus **aroma**!

Other factors supporting the above are **visual appeal, sound (sizzle), anticipation/emotion/comfort**.

The **mouth** observes temperature, texture, piquancy (spiciness), and astringency (pucker/tannin), and through the taste buds: sweetness, saltiness, sourness, bitterness, and umami.

The **nose** registers aroma, pungency, and chemestesis (tingle).

The **eyes** see steam, shades, colour, contrast, and dimensions.

The **ears** hear the sizzle, the popping and the cracking of ice in a drink.

Menu Layout

Front cover, or top or bottom of the menu: Name or pictorial display to create a relationship between the guest and the establishment.

Institutional copy: A mission or comfort statement identifying the philosophy, or the purpose or history of the establishment. This could contain a promotional summary of key employees such as the chef's experience, the skills of the mâitre'd (host) or the sommelier (wine waiter) or the owner. Commonly an illustration is used on a themed menu.

Headings: Grouping the listed menu items in sequence of consumption.

Menu items' description: Can be applied in many ways: with a classical name, committing to classically established procedures, or with the name of the main item such as cut of beef (sirloin steak) or combining the type and name of the dish (lentil soup). There are no rules on how the menu item is described as long as the rules from 1 to 7 as described earlier are respected. Most guests appreciate a short and to the point description allowing them to navigate through the menu with ease. However, if the description is too vague and does not sufficiently reveal the ingredients, customers may move to the next item they can relate to. If the description is too lengthy, it might be too cumbersome to read and to remember.

How Many Menu Items Should a Restaurant Menu Offer?

There is no easy answer; it mainly depends on the concept and theme. An Asian restaurant, by tradition, is expected to have a lengthy menu; in comparison, a steak house or themed restaurant usually offers a short menu. Most others are somewhere in between.

The sample menu on page 53 offers a total forty-six items, not including side dishes, which should be sufficient to satisfy most guests' expectations.

The right balance is usually found by carefully monitoring popularity and finding out why items are or are not popular—listening to customer's preferences and periodically performing a **menu analysis**.

Points to consider: The more extensive the menu, the more time a customer will need to make a decision, which could lead to lost sales. Management of the kitchen also becomes more challenging. The skill and numbers of staff will be in direct proportion with preparations for offered menu items. Product on hand will need to be carefully monitored for appropriate levels, not to be over- or under-stocked, production and holding equipment will have to be available to handle the multitude of items.

> *The 80/20 rule, meaning that in anything a few (20 percent) are vital and many (80 percent) are trivial, also known as Pareto's principle, applies to menus too.*

Pareto's principle, or Pareto's law as it is sometimes called, can be a very effective tool to help you manage effectively.

American menu expert Banger Smith, who has evaluated hundreds of menus, says that regardless of the number of menu items in a specific category like appetizers or entrées, the top three to four sellers consistently account for 60 percent or more of each category's sales.

He questions, and I concur: Why have ten or twelve appetizers when six or eight will satisfy the vast majority of your customers and will generate virtually the same amount of sales?

Look at the sales mix in each section of the menu. The number and extent of unpopular items on your menu will become very apparent. Simplify your kitchen by dropping some of your slow sellers, especially if they contain ingredients that aren't used in other items. That will reduce the number of products to purchase and to maintain in inventory. Chances are, very few, if any, customers will notice, and it may greatly simplify the management of your kitchen, reducing the number of food items to be purchased, stored, and inventoried.

Who Should the Menu Be Written for?

What age group and disposable income does your demographic reveal?

From a marketing perspective, age groups are divided into four key groups:

18 to 29, 30 to 49, 50 to 64, and 65 plus. There are subgroups depending on what product is marketed: 8 to 14, 15 to 24, 25 to 34, and 75 to 84. Being aware of and understanding these divisions makes it quite easy to select a target group or groups.

By statistics, the middle-aged group spends the most money on entertainment and restaurants. If children and grandparents are welcome, perhaps combining two or three groups will attract the clients the marketing area offers. I read a forecast that in Toronto by 2021 the population will be 6.4 million and 16 percent (1.02 million) will be 65 plus and retired. Another study suggested that by 2010 to 2015 there will be more dependent adults than dependent children in Canada.

A restaurant menu should be more than just a list of food with prices; it is a reflection of your restaurant type, style, concept, and atmosphere. As previously mentioned, the menu is one of the primary marketing tools and warrants consideration. There are three main parts to designing a restaurant menu: layout, description, and pricing.

Menu Layout

Design, Colours and Fonts, Borders and Paper

The restaurant menu design is the first impression of the restaurant for the potential customer. The font and colour scheme should reflect your restaurant theme. For example, if you are opening an Italian-themed restaurant, vibrant colours such as red, olive green, purple, and golden yellow would be good choices for a menu. These same colors would look out of place on the menu of a French bistro where dark red and blue should be predominant. The same applies to fonts. A French bistro may use a classic script font or simple plain font, while a pub or other casual restaurant might have a less formal or humorous font. Select a font that is easy to read and not too small. Consider the light in the establishment and the age of your potential customers. Also to consider is the monetary importance of the listed item. **Changing the font** to a larger size or *italic*, or if the writing is confined within boxes/borders, a different *font-type is unusual*, but also acceptable. The attention drawn to a menu item should be in direct proportion with money (gross profit) made. It goes without saying that there is a considerable difference in the contribution margin of a soup in comparison to a coffee, yet very often the same size font is used.

Borders, formal or informal, can be used to enhance the available print area and add a touch of class. Page borders must be carefully selected and should be discreet.

The quality of the selected paper stock for the printed menu may increase or decrease the perceived image of the establishment. There are many types of paper available, from silky smoothness to coarse textured, from dull to shiny, from transparent to opaque, from brilliant white to off-white, to any colour you can imagine. If the menu page is inside a sleeve or holder or laminated and the customer will not come in direct contact with the paper, then quality and colour of the paper is not as important; however, if the printed page(s) is/are unprotected, then the paper's feel (texture) will leave an impression. To select a paper stock, it is advisable to obtain a variety of finishes and colours, print a sample menu, and observe under different lighting conditions the readability of the print in your establishment. Examples of paper colours and contrasting ink colour effects can be seen on www.menuforprofit.com

Menu and Menu Item Description

Menus do not need to be literary creations. Effective menus use uncomplicated yet informative descriptions for each item, creating excitement and encouraging the guest to order the item. Remember the five senses and rules 1 to 7. Explain the key ingredients of a particular dish, the prep and cooking methods, and the flavour sensation. Describe the aroma, the presentation, and, if appropriate, the sizzle, so that the guest can draw an accurate mental picture of what to expect. To follow through with the actual presentation is a must. Usage of foreign or ethnic names is appropriate as long as there is an English or French explanation, depending where in Canada the establishment is located.

My favourite method: Page 51

I draw an outline of the plate(s) to be used and all components of the proposed dish based on the standard recipes, including garnishes, identifying all colours, textures, portion size in proportions, and the intended presentation (layout). Once this is completed, to prepare a menu description is rather easy and it is unlikely that something gets forgotten.

See examples on pages 51 to 55

Menu Pricing

Standard recipes, expected gross profit, associated food and labour cost, and portion control are effective ways to help price a menu correctly, in order to make the expected profit. Care must be taken to be competitive within the local market.

Menu mix, sales mix, or popularity index (all three are basically the same) should be used to ensure a good mix of pricy and economical items with a stable cost and limited use of market price items, which have the greatest fluctuation in cost.

Specialty Restaurant Menus

Create a specialty menu for holidays, local festivals, or events. Mother's Day, being one of the busiest days in the restaurant industry, along with New Year's Eve and Valentine's Day, are prime examples for a specialty menu instead of or in addition to the regular restaurant menu. Specialty menus, table d'hôte, and prix fixe menus allow you to offer your regular diners a different selection while still maintaining, or even lowering, food and labour cost due to limited selection and ease of preparation. For these and other special occasions it may be advantageous to offer two to three seatings, allowing 1½ to 2 hours for each, e.g., brunch and lunch starting at 10 AM and dinner starting at 4 PM.

Changing the Menu

In order to excite guests and staff, and to remain a competitive restaurant, menus should be updated, flexible, and feature specials.

The reason for changing a menu should be to capture new prospective diners and keep them patronizing the restaurant while retaining successful, by profitability and popularity, signature dishes.

After a new opening, changes in the demographics, ownership, or key staff, allow several weeks to let patrons get familiar with the current offerings, survey and listen to them, experiment with different ideas, and watch their performance closely. Monitor changed items at different times of the day and different meal periods. If the appetizers are selling better at lunch than at dinner, there are definite reasons: cost, portion size, menu item description are just a few.

Ultimately, diners determine what works and what doesn't based on their willingness to buy menu items.

Changing an entire menu may not be effective. Regular customers patronize the establishment for a reason. They probably have personal favourites and may not come back if they are no longer available.

Also, changing an entire menu may not be efficient; many hidden costs are associated with changing your menu, including testing and tasting new recipes, reprinting the menu, retraining your staff (both kitchen and floor), reprogramming your ordering system, and re-evaluating your processes.

Added benefits of changing the menu are that staff will be excited and challenged by the change. Care must also be taken that the established labour requirements and subsequent costs are not exceeded and that the new menu items do not go beyond the capacity of the staff and the equipment.

Promoting Preferred and/or High Profit Margin Items

Offer items at a discount, hoping to increase customer counts and increase profits. Create a regular weekly schedule for specials (Monday is XY special day, for example) so regular diners know what to expect and put it on their calendar.

My Favourite Method

Menu item description process for a four-course menu:

Appetizer: *Hot,* ***Soup:*** *Cold,* ***Main:*** *Hot,* ***Dessert:*** *Warm*

Three plates, one bowl, plates uniform or different shapes. Plate colour and design: Plain white, various shapes, and a standard recipe for each course.

Appetizer: Shrimp, Scallops, Orange Ginger Sauce (Contemporary), ecipe created by my friend and colleague Jürgen Lindner, published in On Cooking, Fourth Canadian Edition, Pearson Education Canada, ISBN-13:978-0-13158821-9, page 488. Reprinted with permission.

Soup: Watermelon, Tomato, Cold, Recipe from Food & Diet, June 2009

Main: Chicken Coconut Curry, Shiitake, Basmati Rice, Bok choy, Peanuts, recipe from LCBO Food & Drink Magazine, Early Summer 2009, page 176

Dessert: Savarin (Rum Baba), French: Classic—Baba au rhum, recipe from On Cooking, page 886

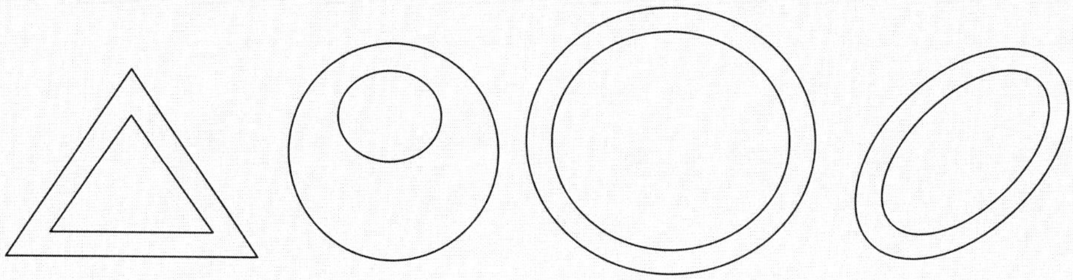

Appetizer *Soup* *Main* *Dessert*

(Continued)

Ingredient	Prep-Cook	Colour	Flavour	Alerts
Sautéed	Scallops and	**Shrimps with**	**Orange Ginger**	**Sauce**
Scallops 20/30	Fresh-sauté	White	Mild	Mollusk
Shrimp 21/25	Fresh-sauté	Pink/white	Mild	Shellfish
Shallots	Fresh, brunoise	Green/white	Mild	Onion
Garlic	Fresh, minced	White	Medium	Garlic
Butter	Fresh	White/nutty	Mild	Dairy
S & P			Mild to strong	Sodium
Orange Ginger	**Sauce**			
Butter	Fresh	White/nutty	Mild	Dairy
Shallots	Fresh, brunoise	Green/white	Mild	Onion
Garlic	Fresh, minced	White	Medium	Garlic
Ginger	Fresh, purée	Creamy	Strong	Ginger
Bay leaf	Dried	Green/removed	Mild	Seasoning
Orange juice	Concentrated	Orange	Tangy/medium	Citrus/acetic
Wine, white	Un-cork	White to green	Dry to sweet	Alcohol
Fish stock	F/F	White/cream	Mild	Fish
Cream 35%	Fresh	White	Mild	Dairy
Juice from sautéed scallops and shrimps		nutty	Mild	Shellfish
Brioche loaf plain	OC page 795	Toasted	Sweet/mild	Yeast

Method of preparation:

Scallops and Shrimps (1) Sweat shallots and garlic in butter, then increase heat and sauté scallops and shrimps for 1 minute. (2) Reserve sautéed items in a warm place. Reserve juice from sautéed shrimp and scallops for sauce.

Orange-Ginger Sauce (1) Melt butter in saucepan and sweat shallots, garlic, and ginger. (.) Add bay leaf, orange juice, white wine, and fish stock and simmer for approximately 30 minutes (3) Add cream and reserved shellfish juice. (4) Adjust seasoning with salt and pepper (5) Remove bay leaf and blend sauce with hand mixer. (6) Strain through a fine strainer and keep warm.

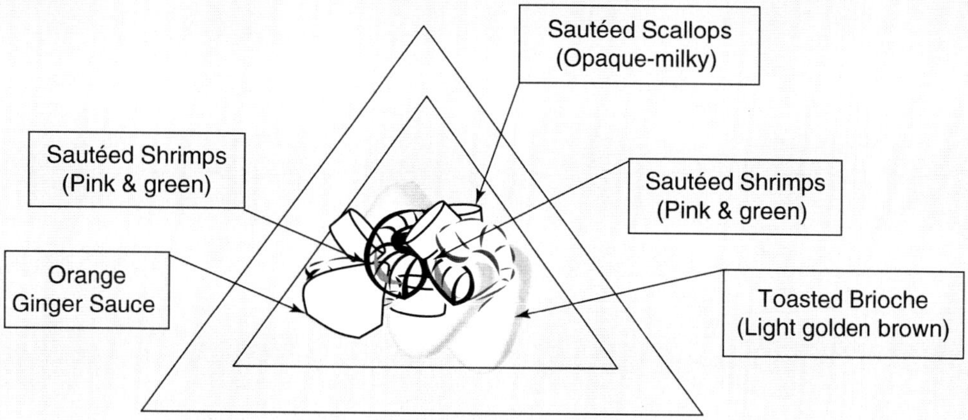

Presentation: *The scallop and shrimp are presented on a triangular plate partially atop toasted focaccia bread slices and napped with the orange-ginger sauce.*

Descriptions for this dish are based on the following facts and features:

Toasted brioche bread*—crisp, buttery, rich taste. . . .*

Scallops*—fresh from, type or size, region, sea (largest) or bay (smallest), tender, sweet, cooked in. . . . For scallops and the shrimp, size is important—larger more succulent and more expensive. If Canadian, this should be mentioned.*

Shrimp*—fresh from Gulf white, pinks, or browns, and black tiger, size from titi (90 to 400) to extra-colossal (8 or less per lb), warm or cold water, fresh water prawns, marine water (salty) shrimp, peeled and deveined, cooked in its reduction. . . .*

The fact that the shrimps are peeled and deveined is a selling feature on a medium-priced menu; on a high-priced menu it is expected.

Orange Ginger Sauce*—fresh ginger, white wine (dry to sweet, name of wine), reduction, rich (creamy), orange juice concentrated, tangy. . . .*

Writing considerations:
Heading: APPETIZERS

Key feature = Scallop and Shrimp

(Continued)

Name of dish:
Fruits de mer (Foreign, needs explanation in English)

The best from the sea (awakens interest but is not descriptive)

Orange and ginger sauce glazed scallops and shrimp (items to be sold are scallops and shrimp, not orange and ginger)

Scallops and shrimp glazed with an orange and ginger reduction on toasted brioche slices (bare minimum: obviously not cooked, good for naming the standard recipe, but does very little to "sell" the dish)

Judge the three different writing styles:

Description one:

Sautéed Scallops and Shrimp
on toasted brioche
napped with an orange, wine, and ginger reduction

Description one:
Sight—NO, Taste—NO, Touch-bite—NO, Smell—NO, Hearing—NO
Rule 1. NO, 2. NO, 3. N/A, 4. YES, 5. YES, 6. NO, 7. Hint

Description two:

Bay of Fundy Scallops and Black Tiger Shrimp
sautéed in butter with shallots and garlic
napped with an orange, dry white wine, and ginger reduction
presented on a lightly toasted brioche

Description two:
Sight—NO, Taste—Hint, Touch-bite—NO, Smell—NO, Hearing—NO
Rule 1. Hint, 2. Hint, 3. N/A, 4. YES, 5. YES, 6. Hint, 7. YES

Description three:

Scallops and Shrimp
Bay of Fundy scallops, paired with extra large black tiger shrimp
sautéed in butter with garden-fresh shallots and garlic,
on a lightly toasted homemade brioche,
napped with a tangy orange concentrate, dry white wine, and ginger reduction

> ***Description three:***
> *Sight—Hint, Taste—Hint, Touch-bite—NO, Smell—NO, Hearing—NO*
> *Rule 1. Hint, 2. Hint, 3. N/A, 4. YES, 5. YES, 6. YES, 7. YES*
> *My opinion: Description one: insufficient,*
> *Description two: acceptable*
> *Description three: Too much unnecessary information*
> *Your opinion?:*______________________________

Menu item descriptions should not contain the following characters: **#, %, &, +, \, w/**—minimize the use of "and, with" as much as possible.

Capitalization of Words

Many documents, including menus, suffer from over-capitalization. The writer sprinkles capitals everywhere in an attempt to make words stand out—with the result that nothing stands out. Here are some simple rules to help you avoid this common offence.

- Capital letters are mainly used to begin a sentence, for the names of **specific** people, organisations, and places. (**Note:** When you use these titles in sentences, you do not capitalize the word *the* that precedes the name.)
- **Geographical places:** Australia, Paris, the North Pole, Beardy Street, the Nepean River, Byron Bay
- **Languages and nationality:** I speak "name your languages." We must learn from the many strengths of Aboriginal learning styles.

Note: The difference between the general use (uncapitalized) and the specific instance (capitalized).

- **Days, months, and seasons**—Friday, September. Seasons are not capitalized: spring, summer, fall and winter
- **Historical events and periods**—the Second World War, the Depression, the Renaissance
- **Capitalize brand names but not products.**

Example: Heinz, Hellman, Grey's Dijon mustard
Do not capitalize words like ketchup or rice.

- **Noun**—A word that names a person, place, thing, or idea. Only proper nouns are capitalized.
- Verb—A word that expresses action or state of being and that tells what the subject of the clause is or does. Verbs are not capitalized.

Here are common menu-writing mistakes:

- Writing menu items names that fail to focus on the key ingredient.
- Creating content without focus—description of methods, side dishes, sauces, and presentation are more embellished than the key ingredient.
- Using too many words, too few details, or no focus on the five senses and the seven rules.

Menu writing is a fine art.

The menu item description needs to identify the main ingredient.

But some description go on like this: *Black Angus dry aged ribeye steak, Sonoma cabernet jus, fresh rosemary, in-house-dried crèpes, carefully roasted pine nuts, grilled locally grown scallions, roasted garlic fingerling potatoes, and wilted greens.* Too much is too much.

Keep it simple:

Black Angus charcoal-grilled ribeye steak
with a boletus mushroom and pine nut Sonoma reduction.
Garlic mashed potatoes and wilted greens

A bit more about creative writing.

I went to a nice vegetarian restaurant the other night and had the Shahkloot special. Specifically, I had crosnes, feta cheese, tabouleh, Greek olives, cucumber, avocado, hummus, falafel, and fresh herbs. Normally, I would not have ordered a dish like this—way too much on the plate—but I was interested in the crosnes, a word or item I had not heard the name of or seen before. Although I asked the server about it and did not receivesatisfactory answer, I ordered it away.

Crosnes, it turns out, are small larva-shaped vegetables, better known as Chinese artichokes, crunchy and not much else. They did very little in the dish, but on the menu, they had done an excellent job of awakening my interest.

Menu language, with its hyphens, quotation marks, and random usage of foreign words, serves less to describe food than to stimulate expectations. Take the description of my dish above: It promises the unconventional crosnes, combined with familiar items like hummus, falafel—then coats it with a thin façade of glamour. This menu entry didn't merely enticed me, it sold me.

Not every menu manipulates the customer in the same way. Different kinds of restaurants use different strategies. Here's a guide to some of the most popular.

- **Hand-holding:** Many chain restaurants deal with novice and hesitant eaters. Their menus aim for reassurance. Despite the "fun" names for dishes, "Scampi in love," "Death by Chocolate," menu language at most chain restaurants is extravagantly specific. It dictates the exact weight of a steak, the number of popcorn shrimp on a platter, and how many slices of bacon will top a bacon cheeseburger. For more precision still, many chain restaurants put pictures of their offerings on the menu, something that is never seen in more upscale restaurants. The hand-holding guarantees the worried diner that there will be no surprise here.

- **Over the top:** As dining gets finer, menu language graduates from reassuring to pretentious. There is a certain class of adjective that appears on restaurant menus and almost nowhere else: roasted, crisped, seared, and glazed, often hyphenated, for emphasis, with the likes of pan, oven, steam, maple, and honey. These adjectives are often applied to staple basic ingredients like a chicken breast: hazelnuts, bacon, foie gras, and, prime among them, truffle oil.

  Fresh imported truffles themselves still sell for hundreds of dollars a kilo, but byproducts like truffle oils and butters have mainstreamed the concept into the adjective "truffled." Nobody looks twice at celeriac on a menu, but a truffled celeriac: Now, that's a different story. Food offered on over-the-top menus may or may not be exceptional. What's certain is that this restaurant thinks that it impresses you.

- **Traffic jamming:** Menus tend to be simpler abroad because other cultures have dishes that are historically established as theirs. Everyone in Italy knows what saltimbocca is. You don't have to tell a Frenchman what's in a gratin dauphinoise. But for better and for worse, North American chefs aren't obliged to culinary history. Instead, some menus are written to make common basic menu items like "Spaghetti with tomato sauce" appear to be "Spaghetti with plum tomatoes, garlic, extra virgin olive oil, and fresh chili flakes." Writing a menu this way caters to the particular expectations of certain North American diners. This may inadvertently lead diners to micromanage their meal, picking and choosing among the ingredients.

  Traffic-jamming menus exist in part to convince diners that they could not replicate such dishes at home, because of the number of components on a plate and the time it takes to make. It makes the diner believe that he or she is getting his or her money's worth. For instance, the offering from a unnamed hotel: "Herb basted loin of venison, maple-glazed endive, vanilla-seasoned spiced sweet yam purée, dark chocolate venison reduction, and glazed cranberries." Now, who would try to make "dark chocolate venison reduction" at home?

- **Freshening up:** I have read many menus where, it seems, they use the word "fresh" with almost everything. A reputable place should not need to point out that the food is fresh. Do I need to assume that if the word "fresh" is not used that the menu item may not be fresh?

- **Branding:** Other menus I have read list the brand name of ingredients like "Keens mustard, Lactantia butter, Renée's salad dressings" or the farmers' names from whom they obtain their ingredients, menus to recognize the farmers and suppliers who have a special relationship with the establishment or to imply quality standards. Using name of regions or farmers may indicate to the reader that the chef is concerned about the carbon footprint and adheres to the 100-mile rule; however, using this information in menu item descriptions may make for cumbersome reading, especially for patrons not familiar with the area.

- **Glamorizing the written word:** Most North American menus are written in English; however, some chefs can't resist using foreign words like "onion soup au gratin, frog legs Provençal, or artichokes velouté." These words may intimidate some customers while the more adventurous ones may ask the server for an explanation, which in turn may lead into a chance to up-sell. Menu glamorizing isn't always foreign: "Emulsions, infusions, and foams" have institutional appeal, whereas "house or homemade chorizo (Spanish style sausage) goat cheese, smoked salmon, vinegars, prosciutto" (Italian-style cured pork ham) suggests that the "house" is making these items from selected raw products with care and know-how.

- **Bare minimum:** Some chefs prefer non- florid menu descriptions, focusing on the key-elements of the dish, like "Classic Osso Buco." This "less is more" approach to writing might be OK with customers who eat out all the time, but it may alienate others. New customers probably would like to have an explanation for "Classic," provided they know what an osso buco is, and most likely they also want to know what else is served with it.

- **The non-menu menu:** When I worked in one ritzy New York restaurant, the servers would go running when a certain oil billionaire/power broker strolled into the place and ordered his special Atlantic Lobster salad—the one that was not on the menu. As any aspiring kingpin knows, true restaurant power means never having to read the menu.

TABLE 5 The Good, the Not-So-Good and the Bad Words in Menu writing (author's opinion) If you have any suggestions for in- or exclusions," please send them to etservice1978@gmail.com Thank you.

THE GOOD	THE NOT SO GOOD	THE BAD
Aged (Beef, Game, Wine)	A la (unless appropriate)	Accented
Al dente	And (use sparingly)	Accompanied (by/with)
Alternative selection	Any style	Any abbreviation (w/ &)
Aromatic	Authentic (it must be true)	Appetizing
Authentic (if it's true)	Baby (if unavoidable)	Arranged
Bite size	Bland	Assorted
Blend, blended	Chunks-chunky	BBQ
Bouquet	Composed-combined	Bed (on a, in a, under)
Brand descriptor (Tabasco)	Concocted-Concoction	Bountiful
Candied	Cooked in	Coated with
Chilled	Cuts (Macédoine, Brunoise)	Complemented
Classic	Dash	Composed
Coated, Covered	Delectable	Covered, with, covering,
Colour descriptors	Delicate	Crowned
Consistency described (light)	Delicious	Dainty
Cooking methods (any & all)	Deluxe	Dazzle-dazzling
Creamy-smooth	Devine	Delightful
Crisp(y)	Dipped, drippings, dressing	Drenched, Dunked
Cuts (Julienne, sliver, thin)	Dollop	Either, or
Decadent	Drizzled	Embellished
Delicacy	Enveloped	Embraced
Enriched	Exceptional-ly	Encircled-enclosed
Essence	Exotic (if not)	Enhanced
Flaky (used appropriately)	Exquisite	Escorted
Folded-wrapped	Favourite (yours, mine)	Extra (everything)
Fragrant	Fancy (unless grade)	Fluffy
Free range (if it's true)	Filled with	Fresh (freshest)

Freshly (squeezed)
Fused-infused-fusion of
Glazed
Golden (yellow-brown)
Grass fed (if it's true)
Herbed
Hint
Imported (from where)
Hot (steaming/burning hot)
Light—Airy
Marinated in/with
Market or Garden fresh
Meatless
Mild, Spicy
Napped
Organic (if it's true)
Origin descriptor (i.e. Canadian)
Original (must be true)
Paired
Piquant
Product type descriptor
Reduction—reduced in/with
Refreshing
Robust
Rolled
Savoury
Scented
Seasonal—in season
Selected
Silky
Sizzling
Slow—cooked
Smoked (hot—cold)
Smoked (type of wood)

Fine, finest
Finished (with)
Flavoured
Flavourful
Garnished (try not to use)
Gently
Home Style-Homemade
In harmony
Hot from the oven
Irresistible
Jumbo (unless Shrimp)
Layered
Mature
Nutritious (unless explained)
Old fashioned
Our very own
Piping hot

Pleasing
Plump
Rich
Scrumptious
Stuffed with
Tenderized
Tidbit
To perfection (subjective)
To your liking-order
Topped
Ultimate
Unusual
With (use sparingly)

Full flavoured
Gathered-Gathering
Gigantic
Good value
Gourmet
Gracious
Gratifying
Heaped-helping
Heart warming
In a dressing, emulsion, jus
Incredible
Liberal (i.e. serving)
Luscious-lush
Luxurious
Marvellous
Mixture
Moistened

Mound
Mouth-watering
Nested
On (a) anything
Overflowing
Palatable
Perfect
Pivoted
Placed
Pleasant-pleasing
Plenty
Puddle
Quaint
Secret (Ingredient, Recipe)
Sensational
Served in: Gravy, Dressing
Served with-on

(Continued)

TABLE 5 *(Continued)*

THE GOOD	THE NOT SO GOOD	THE BAD
Soft		Smothered
Style (in reference to)		Sprinkled with-on
Sumptuous-Succulent		Superb
Sun dried-ripened		Surrounded with-by
Tantalizing		Symphony
Tangy		Tantalizing
Tender		Tasty-tasteful
Traditional (if it is)		To die for
Tropical		To your liking
Unique (if it is)		Towering
Vine ripened		Wonderful
Wrapped		Young
Zesty		Zippy
ADD YOUR OWN WORDS:		

Demographic Studies, Psychographics, and Competitive Analysis

Chapter 6

Feasibility study: Will the theme and concept be profitable based on the selected demographic area?

As mentioned in the introduction, I will not describe in great detail their functions. Although very important functions, they are best left to experts because of their complexity and possible errors in interpretation.

Demographic study: A study of a specific area, location, and its population for various evaluation purposes.

The result of this study should reveal the statistical information of populations with reference to size, density, distribution, and vital statistics as well as the ability (of the current market) to expand or decline.

Demographics are prepared for many different reasons. For the purpose of establishing a restaurant or other food service establishment, the following is perhaps the most important information about the population. The research process is referred to as **psychographics** or **customer profiling**:

- Age
- Ethnic origin
- Household type
- Marital status
- Occupation
- Income and disposable income
- Number of vehicles per family
- Who are my potential customers?
- Would they fit my planned concept?
- Where are my customers coming from?
- What do they have in common?
- What activities are they participating in/patronizing?
- Other related data

What is my personal knowledge of the area?

The following information is evaluated for estimating the success (feasibility) of a specific type of establishment:

- What is the potential of a population increase in this area?
- What could be my share of the market? (based on direct or indirect competition)

- What is the mix of residential, commercial, and/or manufacturing properties?
- Does this area have any attractions?
- Public transportation, ease of access, parking?
- How much area do I need for the planned business to succeed?
- How many potential customers could be attracted by the planned concept?

And perhaps most important for planning a specific type of establishment is the knowledge of **disposable income.**

Sample Demographic: A Neighborhood Mall in Canada

INFORMATION AT A GLANCE:
Strategically located at highway this mall is a well-established community centre, with a wide selection of strong performing fashion, specialty, and service retailers.

Type of Center: *single level, enclosed*
GLA of Center: *380,000 square feet*
Number of Stores: *105 stores and services*
Parking: *1917 parking stalls*

Demographic Profile: *Trade Area: 5 km radius*

2006 Trade Area Population: 240,406
2010 Trade Area Projected Population: *276,467; anticipating a 15% increase*
Ethnicity: *(top five single responses)*

*English**	*59.8%*	*Polish*	*9.6%*
Italian	*9.2%*	*Portuguese*	*5%*
Ukrainian	*3.9%*		

**English includes: Canadian, English, British, Irish, Scottish, Welsh origins*

Age Breakdown (in Years):

0 to 4	*6%*
5 to 19	*17%*
20 to 24	*6%*
25 to 34	*15%*
35 to 44	*13%*
45 to 54	*13%*
55 to 64	*10%*
65 to 74	*10%*
75 & over	*6%*

2006 Estimated Average Household Income in Trade Area: $79,108

2010 Estimated Average Household Income in Trade Area: $89,037 based on a 3% annual increase.

Estimated weekly traffic: 90,000 shoppers per week (annual average)

Based on the listed facts, what type of restaurant could be opened in the mall? A lot more information is needed. However, the provided information, although a crude assessment of the area, is a good overview.

Once the demographic study is completed, the psychographic and competitive analysis as well as the feasibility study indicate that based on the selected theme and concept, the expected profit is achievable.

A **competitive analysis** or **comparative analysis** will help you realize who your competition might be. Although competition is healthy since it provides an opportunity for price-value relationship and promotion of quality product, I believe it is important to differentiate your establishment's image and/or offerings from the competition to avoid direct competition.

In a competitive environment a business must excel in comparison to the competition to be successful.

Share the market—Market shares

It has become very popular for competitive establishments to congregate within a few blocks from one another, attracting customers to this area and giving them the opportunity to decide which one to patronize.

A list of potentially direct and indirect competitive establishments in alphabetical order:

Asian restaurant: Buffet or table service, specializing in cuisines from the Asian region, including China, Japan, Malaysia, Thailand, Vietnam.

Australian restaurant: Offers a menu characterized by fresh seasonal produce and dishes that reflect trends in Australian cooking, in an informal setting.

Bistro Restaurant: The term *bistro* is sometimes interchanged with *café*. A bistro in its true sense is actually a **café** that offers full meals and service and often features an outdoor patio.

Brasserie: see Bistro Restaurant

Breakfast Restaurant: Specializing in providing breakfast at least six days per week and/or all-day breakfast.

Buffet Restaurant: Often featuring ethnic specialities, especially popular are Oriental, Italian, and Mexican buffets.

BYO Restaurant: Restaurant and bistro that are liquor licensed, allowing customers to bring their own wine. Corkage is usually charged to cover the labour cost and glassware use.

Café: A café is a casual restaurant with an unhurried atmosphere that may or may not offer table service. Customers order their food from a counter and serve themselves or are served. A café menu traditionally offers things such as coffee, espresso, pastries, sandwiches, or light meals. A popular feature of a café is that it often features outdoor seating.

Casual Dining: Offers comfortable atmospheres and has mid-range prices.

Caterer: Caters on-site or off-site and may provide **personal chef services**.

Coffee Shop: Provides coffee, tea, pastries, snacks, and casual meals during day time.

Concessions: Operate in conjunction with other activities such as sporting events, local festivals, or may be seasonal in nature and operate at public parks and pools. Menus are limited and food preparation is simple. Toronto recently licensed concessions; food carts named "Toronto a la cart," which offer ethnic specialities.

Delicatessen: Operation offering foods intended for immediate consumption. The main product line is normally luncheon meats, cheeses, and preserved fish products. Offerings include sandwiches, soups, and salads, crudites, and party trays. Most foods are precooked prior to delivery. Preparation of food products is generally simple, but can also be exclusive and exquisite, catering to the wealthy.

Ethnic Restaurant (see **Specialty Restaurant):** Ranges from quick-service to upscale. Menus usually include North American versions of ethnic dishes and/or authentic ethnic foods often offering kosher and/or Halal products.

Eatertainment Restaurant: A phrase coined for restaurants that rely heavily on entertainment to attract customers, often not focusing on repeat customers and quality food preparation. (Hard Rock Cafe, Planet Hollywood) see also **Restaurant in a Theatre**.

European Restaurant: Specializing in cuisine from a country or region of Europe.

Family Restaurant: Offers a varied menu, including children's menu, and targeted to the family dining market. Since they charge reasonable prices, they also appeal to seniors. They have fast service falling between quick service and full-service restaurants.

Fast Casual Dining: One example of a successful current trend. Fast casual is slightly more upscale than fast food. Fast casual restaurants offer disposable dishes and flatware, but their food tends to be presented as more upscale, such as gourmet breads and organic ingredients. Open kitchens are popular with fast casual chains, where customers can see their food being prepared.

Fast Food: Operations that specialize in one or two main entrees such as hamburgers, pizza, or chicken. These operations may also provide salad and/or ice cream service. Preparation of food products is generally simple and often involves deep-fried food products.

Fine Dining Restaurant: Provides a formal, structured dining experience at the high end of the market. Also referred to as "white tablecloth dining".

French Restaurant: Specialising in French cuisine (although it falls into the European category, it is honourably mentioned separately due to France's long history in organising, standardising, and modernising classical cooking).

Full Service Restaurant: Operations that offer complete and varied menus for breakfast, lunch, and dinner. It usually has multiple entrees for each meal period, which may include soups, salads, and/or desserts. Preparation of food products is often complex and involves multiple steps. Most full-service operations will provide customer seating and may include liquor service (Milestones, Montana, Jack Astor, Outback, just to name a few).

Game Restaurant: Common as in Europe where the gaming and subsequent hunting laws are quite different than in North America. In North America all game to be sold in a restaurant must come from a controlled farming environment. Hunted game may only be served for fundraising purposes.

Ice Cream Parlour: Originated in Europe, evolved to also serve drinks and coffees besides the selection of different homemade ice creams in a similar make up as a café. Usually not found in its traditional style in North America, except in Italian areas of larger cities. North American substitutes, usually without any seating, are places like Baskin & Robbins, Dairy Queen, Ben & Jerry's.

Indian Restaurant: Specializing in regional or general Indian cuisine.

Mexican Restaurant: Specializing in Mexican or Tex-Mex cuisine.

Mobile Unit: Operations that operate from mobile vans, push carts, or trailers selling food items (potentially hazardous). The operations may be somewhat seasonal in nature. Food service may be limited with most of the complex food preparation taking place in a commissary. See also **Concession.**

Pizza Restaurant: Pizza is the primary menu feature.

Pub: Short for public house, pubs date back hundreds of years to Europe, especially Great Britain. Pubs have a timeless appeal for their laid-back atmosphere. Brewpubs offer beer made in house, as well as a wide selection of other beers and ales. Pubs can offer full menus, as well as appetizers.

Raw Food Restaurant: A new trend to be watched—food and juices are processed and served in their raw stages, usually made from organically grown products.

Restaurant in a Brewery: Restaurant within or adjacent to the premises of a brewery, most commonly trying to pair its beers with carefully selected entrees. See also **Restaurant in a Winery.**

Restaurant (Children): Catering specifically to kids. See also **Family Restaurants.**

Restaurant in a Hotel: Offering one or more in-house dining facilities ranging from cafeteria style to a "Signature Restaurant."

Restaurant in a Motel/Motor Inn/Guesthouse: Restaurants within a motel/motor inn/guesthouse offering in-house dining.

Restaurant in a Pub/Hotel/Club/Tavern: Restaurant located within a pub hotel/club/tavern offering in-house dining ranging from snack-bar to casual, to fine dining and banquets.

Restaurant in a Spa: Dining facility within a spa expected to serve healthy food choices.

Restaurant in a Resort: A restaurant located within a resort, offering an in-house dining experience influenced by the theme of the resort.

Restaurant in a Theatre: Theatre with dinner prior to the show, usually self-serve buffets. See also **Eatertainment Restaurant** description from above.

Restaurant in a Winery: Restaurant within or adjacent to the premises of a winery, most commonly trying to pair its wines with carefully selected entrees. See also **Restaurant in a Brewery**.

Seafood Restaurant: Specializing in seafood; offers a wide array of fish a nd shellfish prepared in a variety of ways.

Specialty Restaurant: (also see **Ethnic Restaurant)** Specializing in a particular multicultural or religious cuisine not specifically accommodated by any other listed categories. (vegetarian, vegan, etc.)

Steak House, Restaurant: Red meat is primary focus. Usually offering salad bars and other items such as poultry, seafood, and pasta. Most menu offerings are à la carte including side dishes.

Sushi or Oyster Bar: Usually located within a restaurant, supermarket, or delicatessen, serving raw and specialty seafood items.

Themed Restaurant: Part of a chain or franchise that has a distinctive, deliberate and consistent themed image or brand (Red Lobster, Jack Astor, Olive Garden, Mr. Greek, Rainforest Cafe, etc.).

For some extravagantly themed restaurants visit: http://weburbanist.com/2008/08/10/15-of-the-strangest-themed-restaurants-from-buns-and-guns-to-cannabalistic-sushi/

Vegetarian/Vegan Restaurant: Specializing in serving vegan and/or vegetarian dishes.

Vegetarians

Vegetarians and Vegans are two very different groups and occasionally are incorrectly identified. Here are some definitions to help clarify the difference between them. For additional information, please visit **www.vegansociety.com/home.php**

For up-to-date information please visit: **www.vegsoc.org**

In very simple terms: A vegetarian is someone who does not eat meat and in some cases animal products.

Vegetarians may be classified as ovo-vegetarian, may consume eggs but no dairy products. A lacto-vegetarian may consume dairy products but no eggs. A ovo-lacto-vegetarian may consume eggs and dairy products. Semi-vegetarian may define meat as mammalian flesh but may consume fish and/or poultry or occasionally other meats. A pescetarian may consume fish but not meat. The Vegetarian Society considers pescetarians and semi-vegetarians not to be true vegetarians.

Vegans

Vegans promote ways of living free from animal products for the benefit of people, animals, and the environment.

Menu planners and cooks must understand, in very simple terms, that a vegan dish or menu may not contain any meat raw or cooked and any animal by-product. As I stated before, this is very simplified. For the full text please visit the above mentioned website: **www.vegansociety.com/home.php**

Starting an Establishment from Scratch or Purchasing Existing?

There are many considerations, primarily financial, since it is likely that creating a new establishment is customarily less expensive than purchasing an existing one in a comparable location.

Reason being: When purchasing a "going concern," meaning an existing and profitably operating establishment, one not only purchases the tangible facility but also the "intangible asset—goodwill." Goodwill includes right of way, leases, licences, the existing customer base, and the experienced staff. An existing business will have experienced, proven employees who know their jobs and are very likely responsible for the continued success of the restaurant. Although you may not physically (touchable-hands-on) own them, they are part and parcel of the success of this business.

Statistics show that a new start-up business is far more likely to fail than an existing business with a successful history.

For a menu planner this raises important questions:

To change or not to change—that is the question!

Since the purchase was made because it fit within the planned "concept," there should be no immediate changes made to the menu; instead, the quality of the products, the standard recipes, including purchase costs and portion size and the menu selling prices, should be carefully reviewed and evaluated.

It would also be prudent to measure the individual menu item performance for popularity and profitability using a common **menu analysis method** as described in *A Chef's Companion to Cost Control* by Klaus Theyer CCC., current edition, Kendall/Hunt ISBN 978-0-7575-4762-1. Please visit **www.menuforprofit.com** to download a sample template.

Any changes to the existing menu items' selection, quality of products, portion sizes, and selling prices should be implemented gradually. Perhaps the best method to use is to offer one or more daily specials and monitor customer's reactions by soliciting feedback either verbally or through short focused questionnaires.

As the new manager/chef, it would be prudent to introduce your concept philosophy to staff and patrons and perhaps offer a welcome special for a period of time to all customers. If there is room on the menu, an **add-on** or inserted page or a change to the **merchandising copy** is an easy and reasonably inexpensive way of doing business.

Contrary to an existing establishment, a new business is being created and needs to be promoted within the demographic area. Early advertising of what it will offer will start attracting customers. Another quite successful method of soliciting ideas for menu planning is to serve the existing market by contacting the potential customers, either via direct mail by postal and/or zip code, targeted e-mails, social networking sites (Facebook, Twitter), Internet postings, search engines, local newspaper ads, and public postings, asking for their help and input in creating a restaurant styled to their liking and menu offerings that they would expect. Although this action may affect your planned concept, and as long as the changes are not detrimental, it is feedback that should be seriously considered.

Of course, this method of market research has no bearing on concepts that attract customers because of the uniqueness of offerings: the chefs, maître 'd, sommeliers, or the affineurs reputation, the establishment's style, comfort, and location; like Michael Stadtländer's Eigensinn Farm, Mark McEwan's North 44, Michael Bonacini's & Peter Oliver's Canoe or Auberge de pommier, Grant Achatz at Alinea, Ferran Adrià at El Bulli, Susur Lee at Susur's, Domenic Chiaromonte at T2 Restaurant, Brian Morin of the Bier Bistro, or **branded chain restaurants** such as McDonalds, Wendy's, Ruth Chris's Steakhouses, just to name a few.

The Menu and the Law

Chapter 7

The Menu and the Law

The writing of menus, which is a form of advertising, which requires knowledge of laws applicable to the Consumers Protection Act, http://www.e-laws.gov.on.ca/html/statutes/english/elaws_statutes_02c30_e.htm. The Health Canada regulations http://www.hc-sc.gc.ca/ahc-asc/legislation/index-eng.php as well as other Federal, Provincial and Municipal regulations.

"Not knowing the law does not protect the menu writer from prosecution."

The menu and the law: While writing a menu the wording must accurately reflect what the customers can expect — any wording, which potentially misleads the consumers expectation by not delivering what was promised either, verbally, by depiction or in writing may have legal consequences for the establishment and possibly for the writer or the one who actually prepared the meal or beverage.

The following is not a complete list of, or intended to interpret or to explain the various laws and regulations; it is solely an introduction to the existence of laws and regulations.

The Common Law;
http://www.justice.gc.ca/eng/dept-min/pub/just/03.html
http://www.canadiana.ca/citm/specifique/lois_e.pdf

Standard of Liability;
http://www.guildyule.com/cms/images/M_images/pdf/briefing/vjp%20paper.pdf

The Law of Contracts;
http://canadiancontractlaw.com/makingandbreakingcontracts.html

The Law of Negligence;
http://www.lawyersandsettlements.com/lawsuit/negligence.html
http://legal-dictionary.thefreedictionary.com/negligence

The Foods and Drugs Act;
http://laws-lois.justice.gc.ca/eng/acts/F-27/index.html

The Sales of Goods Act;
http://www.canadalegal.com/gosite.asp?s=1880

The Good Samaritan Legislation;
http://www.canadianlawsite.ca/goodsamaritan.htm

Menus and Advertising;
http://www.adstandards.com/en/standards/canCodeOfAdStandards.aspx
http://www.hc-sc.gc.ca/dhp-mps/advert-publicit/index-eng.php
http://www.inspection.gc.ca/food/labelling/guide-to-food-labelling-and-advertising/eng/1300118951990/1300118996556

Religious Dietary Laws
http://www.inspection.gc.ca/english/fssa/labeti/guide/ch4ae.shtml#a4_16

Other areas subsequently affected: Food Standards;
http://www.hc-sc.gc.ca/fn-an/securit/chem-chim/contaminants-guidelines-directives-eng.php

Allergies;
http://www.inspection.gc.ca/about-the-cfia/acts-and-regulations/eng/1299846777345/1299847442232

Substitutions;
http://www.inspection.gc.ca/english/fssa/labeti/guide/ch4ae.shtml

Food Poisoning;
http://www.hc-sc.gc.ca/fn-an/securit/ill-intox/index-eng.php
http://www.inspection.gc.ca/proactive-disclosure/eng/1300126592747/1302475174145

The provided links are for your convenience and were accurate at the time of writing, however, the writer does not claim that all links are provided and suggest consulting with available sources and legal professionals prior to printing a menu for public view.

ACCURACY IN MENUS is covered under:

Federal and Provincial Legislation (False Advertising)
Food and Drugs Act (Labelling)
The Sales of Goods Act ~ Donation of Food Act
Combined Investigations Act

Various liability for Employer and/or Employee — Penalties

1. Summary Conviction: (Misdemeanours), fines up to $5,000, time up to six month in jail.
2. Indictment: No limit on fine, up to five years in jail.

Please review the web-pages containing definition and or explanations for the various laws, regulations and acts.

A menu is a form of advertising:
A menu is an **invitation to do business**. **Offer to do business** is done through various menu presentations (in writing, depicted or verbal).

An offer is based on **provided information** (Restaurant, Menu, Advertising, Web-pages and Staff).

A Contract is entered by the consumer accepting the offer by ordering from the menu(s) and accepting the delivered goods.

Contract = Offer and Acceptance

Introduction

Menu accuracy has long been a major concern of the food service industry. **Consumer satisfaction and goodwill** depend on their faith that menus are represented truthfully.

Customers have the right to expect that menu phrases and terminology, photographs, illustrations and other printed material are accurate. This applies to **verbal depiction** by employees.

Federally, it is the primary responsibility of the **Consumer and Corporate Affairs** department to regulate and **enforce legislation** pertaining to the rights of consumers. Provincial governments have further acts and regulations expanding on specific-areas of representation.

The contents of this section have been developed in consultation with Consumer and Corporate Affairs, Canada. It has been developed to assist the foodservice operator in properly representing foods offered for sale in restaurants.

Representation of Quantity

Any written or pictorial description of net quantity (size, weight, or portion of food) that could deceive the consumer is considered misleading and therefore prohibited. Steaks are customarily merchandised by weight, and the generally accepted practice of **declared quantity is weight prior to cooking.**

If "extra large" eggs are listed, they must be just that, since "extra large" is a **recognized egg size based on weight and grading standards**.

The use of terms such as "extra large salad" or "extra tall drink" or "Lunch and dinner size" may invite problems if not qualified.

There is no question about the meaning of a "3-egg omelette" or "all you can eat" or "5 oz of wine"

Representation of Quality

Federal and provincial grade standards exist for many products sold through restaurants, including eggs, poultry, meat and game meat, dairy products and fresh and processed fruits and vegetables.

Some examples of grade terminology are; Canada extra fancy, Canada fancy, Canada No. 1, Canada choice, Canada grade "AAA", or Prime, etc.

Care must be exercised in preparing menu descriptions when these words are used. **In certain cases, they imply quality**. A beef item appearing as "Canada Prime" connotes the use of Canada Prime grade beef.

The "Food and Drug" definition for regular ground beef excludes the use of extra fat, water, extenders or binders. The fat content is limited to 30%. When seasonings are added, the product must be called seasoned ground beef "or "ground beef with seasoning.

The ***Food and Drugs Act*** in conjunction with the ***Meat Inspection Act*** prescribes the following common names and standards for ground meat. In this respect, it is imperative that a product labelled with a given common name contain **only** that which is allowed by the **corresponding standard**:

COMMON NAME	STANDARD
Extra Lean Ground [naming the species]*	shall be boneless, skinless meat of the species indicated that has been ground and shall not contain more than **10%** fat
Lean Ground [naming the species]*	shall be boneless, skinless meat of the species indicated that has been ground and shall not contain more than **17%** fat
Medium Ground [naming the species]*	shall be boneless, skinless meat of the species indicated that has been ground and shall not contain more than **23%** fat
Regular Ground [naming the species]*	shall be boneless, skinless meat of the species indicated that has been ground and shall not contain more than **30%** fat

Annex 1, *Meat Inspection Regulations*, 1990
*[Naming the species] = beef, pork, chicken, turkey, etc.

It should be noted that the standards provided above do not allow for the addition of:

1. any species other than the species named (e.g. ground pork is not permitted to be added to a product labelled as "lean ground beef");
2. mechanically separated meat;
3. any preservative (e.g. sulphites, sodium erythorbate, ascorbic acid, etc.);
4. any other ingredient or additive (e.g. fillers, seasonings, phosphates, etc.)

Ground meat products that contain fat beyond permitted levels or contain non-permitted substances as described above are in violation of section 5(1) of the *Food and Drugs Act* in that these products are being labelled, packaged, advertised or sold in a manner that is false, misleading or deceptive. Such violations when encountered at retail are subject to investigation and enforcement action by Retail Food Officers of the Canadian Food Inspection Agency.

Representation of Price

If a cover charge or service charge is part of the pricing structure, customers must be appropriately notified. If an additional charge is imposed for requests such as "all white meat," the customer must be informed at the time the request is made.

Representation of Brand Names

A **registered or copy-written trademark or brand name** must not be used generically to refer to a product. Some examples are; Coca Cola, Heinz Ketchup, Kraft Cheese, Miracle Whip, Ritz Crackers etc. In other words, a no name brand or any other cola brand cannot be offered or sold as Coca Cola.

Table containers of condiments and sauces bearing a specific brand name must contain products of that brand.

The "house" brand of a product may be so labelled even when prepared by an outside source, **if its manufacturing was to your specifications**.

Representation of Product Identification

Because of the similarity of many food products, substitutions are often made. These substitutions may be due to seasonal availability, price, non-delivery, or merchandising considerations. If a substitution was made, any changes must be reflected on the presented menu, preferably in writing.

Some examples are:

PRODUCT CLAIMED:	PRODUCT SERVED:
Classical named dish	Use of other ingredients and/or method of cooking not as identified in the classical recipe.
Maple syrup	Maple flavoured syrup
Veal cutlet	Flaked, formed veal cutlet (A veal cutlet is traditionally/by standards cut from a muscle)
Whipped cream	whipped topping
Chicken	Turkey
Veal	Pork
Butter	Margarine
Grand Marnier Cheesecake	Grand Marnier flavouring flavoured Cheesecake
Dover Sole	Other Sole or Sole fillet

Representation of Points of Origin

To advertise on a menu or anywhere else that a product is originally from a specific geographic place or area when it is not, is misrepresentation and therefore prohibited.

Claims of origin of a product may be substantiated by packaging labels, invoices or other documentation provided by your supplier. Mistakes are possible as sources of supply change and availability or product shifts.

Some examples are; Lake Winnipeg gold-eye, Idaho or PEI potatoes, Florida orange juice, Danish blue cheese, Alaskan king-crab, Brome lake ducks, etc.

There is a wide spread use of geographic names used in a generic sense to describe a method of preparation or service. Such terminology is **readily understood and accepted by the customer** and its use is acceptable, provided the products meet with consumer expectations and applicable standards.

Some examples are; French toast, Thousand Island dressing, English muffins, Danish pastries, Swiss steak, Denver sandwiches, Devilled eggs, Sacher torte, Swiss roll, etc.

Representation of Merchandising Terms

Advertising exaggerations are tolerated only if they do not mislead. To use the term "we only use the finest beef" implies beef from Canada "Prime to AAA" grade carcasses. Black Angus, Kobe and others brand names identify the cattle but do not represent a grading standard. However, to the knowing consumer they represent a certain level of quality.

Mistakes are possible in properly identifying steak cuts. There are about 300 officially recognised names for cuts of beef, yet there are app. 1000 names used to market them. Use **standard industry names** consumers recognise.

"Home-style," "homemade style" or "our own" is **suggested terminology** rather than homemade in describing menu offering prepared according to a home recipe.

If any of the following is stated, it **must be able to be** substantiated. The claim: fresh daily, farm fresh, low calorie, Canada's famous, finest quality, etc.

Representation of Means of Preservation

The accepted means of preserving foods are numerous, including canned, chilled, bottled, pickled, frozen and dehydrated and they must be described accurately on your menu. Frozen orange juice is not fresh, canned peas are not frozen, reconstituted or defrosted is not fresh.

Representation of Food Preparation

Accuracy is a must in describing methods of food preparation as this often is a determining factor in entrée selection.

Examples are as follows: charcoal broiled, sautéed, baked, boiled, broiled, roasted, deep fried, barbecued, smoked, prepared from scratch, poached, deep fried in vegetable oil. All listed cooking methods are identified standard methods and often are the key reason for the consumer to select a menu item due to dietary or other health concerns.

Representation of Verbal and Visual Presentation

When your menu or other advertising (insert card, etc.) shows pictorial representation, (graphic illustration design, actual photograph or picture) of a meat or other product, it should accurately portray the actual contents by showing the relative proportion of the individual ingredients present. The phrase "A picture replaces a thousand words" may not apply.

Examples of **visual misrepresentation** include: The use of mushroom pieces in a sauce when the picture depicts mushroom caps, the omission of side-dishes, condiments or other entrée extras when the picture depicts their inclusion, the use of a plain bun when the picture depicts a sesame-topped bun, etc.

Examples of **verbal misrepresentation** include: if the server asks "sour cream or butter with your baked potatoes" when in fact an imitation sour cream or margarine is served.

Representation of Dietary menu items, Nutritional Claims and/or Religious Dietary laws

Some restaurants cater to persons who follow diets or religious dietary laws. Items on the menu that **do not meet the requirements** should be clearly marked. If the menu is ambiguously drafted, an attempt to serve food that has not met the requirements may be **a breach under false advertising and duty of care.**

According to the Food and Drugs Act and Regulations pertaining to nutritional labelling and advertisements, no food may be claimed as being "for special dietary use" by any means whatsoever unless that food is:

a. a carbohydrate-reduced food
b. a sugar-reduced food
c. a calorie-reduced food
d. a low calorie food
e. a low sodium food
f. a formulated liquid diet
g. a food represented for fat-modified diets
h. a food represented for gluten-free diets
i. a food represented for protein-restricted diets
j. a food represented for low (naming the amino acids) diets.

"Low in calories" or "healthy alternative" are nutritional claims, if made, must be supportable by specific data.

Note: Labelling requirements for restaurants are currently considered by several agencies and associations.

Any questions or uncertainties should be discussed with Consumer and Corporate Affairs representatives in order to avoid unintentional breaches of federal regulations.

Federal Food and Drugs Act

Part I of the Federal Food and Drugs Act prohibit the sale, labelling, packaging, processing and advertising of food, drugs, and cosmetics in any manner that is false or misleading. No food may be advertised as a cure or treatment for any of the afflictions listed in the Act. The Act makes it a criminal offense to breach its requirement. Penalties include fines and imprisonment.

Part I, Section 4 and 31 of Canada's Food and Drugs Act states the following:

Section 4

No person shall sell an article of food that;

(a) has in or on it any poisonous or harmful substance;
(b) is unfit for human consumption;
(c) consists in whole or in part of any filthy, putrid, disgusting, rotten, decomposed or diseased animal or vegetable substance;
(d) is adulterated; or
(e) was manufactured, prepared, preserved, packaged, or stored under unsanitary conditions.

Section 31

Every person who contravenes [Part I] or the regulations made under [Part I] is guilty of an offence and is liable

(a) on summary conviction for the first offence to a fine not exceeding five hundred dollars or to imprisonment for a term not exceeding three month or to both and, for a subsequent offence, to a fine not exceeding $5,000 or six month or to both - **and**
(b) on conviction on indictment to a fine not exceeding five thousand dollars or to imprisonment for a term not exceeding three years or to both.

Prosecution under the Food and Drugs Act are undertaken by the crown

The DONATION OF FOOD ACT

Without going into minute details the Federal and the various Provincial Acts dealing with Food Donations and Donated Food Agencies could be summarized to read as follows:

An establishment or a person who donates food or who distributes donated food to another person is not liable for damages resulting from injury or death caused by the consumption of the food unless the food item has contravened the previously mentioned Part I, Section 4 and 31 of the Canada's Food and Drugs Act and/or was intended to cause injury or death or was handled recklessly without regard for the safety of the consumer.

For more detailed information on the Federal act and/or Provincial acts visit:

http://secondharvest.ca/donate-food
http://www.canlii.org/en/nl/laws/stat/snl-1997-c-d-26.1/latest/snl-1997-c-d-26.1.html
https://www.e-laws.gov.on.ca/html/statutes/english/elaws_statutes_94d19_e.htm
http://www.canlii.org/en/ab/laws/stat/rsa-2000-c-c-8/latest/rsa-2000-c-c-8.html

1. **Sale of *Goods Act*,** R.S.O. 1990, c. S.1 - e-Laws - *Ontario*
*www.e-laws.gov.on.ca/html/statutes/.../elaws_statutes_90s01_e.htm*Cached

Part I — Formation of the Contract

Sale and agreement to sell

2. (1) A contract of sale of goods is a contract whereby the seller transfers or agrees to transfer the property in the goods to the buyer for a money consideration, called the price, and there may be a contract of sale between one part owner and another. . . .

Part II — Effects of the Contract

Part III — Performance of the Contract

Duties of seller and buyer

26. It is the duty of the seller to deliver the goods and of the buyer to accept and pay for them in accordance with the terms of the contract of sale. R.S.O. 1990, c. S.1, s. 26. . . .

Part IV — Rights of unpaid seller against the Goods

Part V — Actions for breach of the Contract

Part VI — Supplementary

Seller may maintain action for price

47. (1) Where, under a contract of sale, the property in the goods has passed to the buyer and the buyer wrongfully neglects or refuses to pay for the goods according to the terms of the contract, the seller may maintain an action against the buyer for the price of the goods. . . .

Combines Investigation Act:

The *Combines Investigation Act* was a Canadian Act of Parliament, implemented in 1910, passed in 1923 by MacKenzie King, which regulated certain corporate business practices that were anti-competitive. It prohibited monopolies, **misleading advertising**, bid-rigging, price fixing, and other **means of limiting competition**. It was eventually repealed in July 1986 and replaced with the **Competition Act.**

Competition Bureau Canada

Department of Justice — The Competition Bureau

http://www.competitionbureau.gc.ca/eic/site/cb-bc.nsf/eng/00157.html

The Competition Bureau, as an independent law enforcement agency, ensures that Canadian businesses and consumers prosper in a competitive and innovative marketplace. The Bureau uses its publications to inform Canadians about its activities. They clarify the Bureau's position on issues the public and businesses often ask questions about, and on areas in which the interpretation of the *Competition Act*, the *Consumer Packaging and Labelling Act*, the *Textile Labelling Act* and the *Precious Metals Marking Act* is not easily understood.

http://www.competitionbureau.gc.ca/eic/site/cb-bc.nsf/eng/h_01436.html

Labelling Corner

The *Consumer Packaging and Labelling Act* is a regulatory statute. It requires that prepackaged consumer products bear accurate and meaningful labelling information to help consumers make informed purchasing decisions.

APPLICATION OF LABEL TO PRE-PACKAGED PRODUCT

EXEMPTION FROM NET QUANTITY DECLARATION

EXEMPTION FROM METRIC NET QUANTITY DECLARATION AND TYPE SIZE REQUIREMENT

MANNER OF DECLARING NET QUANTITY

UNITS OF MEASUREMENT

http://www.inspection.gc.ca/english/fssa/labeti/inform/sporte.shtmlfssa/labeti/guide/ch1e.shtml

1.2.1 The *Food and Drugs Act* and the *Food and Drug Regulations*
Subsection 5.(1) of the *Food and Drugs Act* (FDA) prohibits the labelling, packaging, treating, processing, selling or advertising of any food (at all levels of trade) in a manner that is false, misleading or deceptive to consumers or is likely to create an erroneous message regarding the character, value, quantity, composition, merit or safety of the product. Subsections 3(1) and (2) prohibit health claims that might suggest that a food is a treatment, preventative or cure for specified diseases or health conditions, unless provided for in the regulations. . . .

Summary Conviction Offence Definition

In Canada, a less serious offence than indictable offences and for which both the procedure and punishment tends to be less onerous.

Canada, contrary to the United States, did not retain the common distinction between misdemeanors and felonies and, instead, crimes in Canada are classified as either indictable offences or offences punishable on summary conviction, *aka* summary conviction offences.

There are also hybrid offences, which allow the prosecutor to opt between proceedings by way of summary conviction or by indictment.

All summary conviction offences must be tried in what the Canadian Criminal Code, at §785, defines as summary conviction court, usually a lower-level court such as a provincial court, as opposed to a higher court, such as a Supreme or Court of Queen's bench court.

http://www.canlii.org/en/ca/laws/stat/rsc-1985-c-c-46/latest/

COMPARED WITH Indictable Offences

- There is no time limit to when charges can be laid, e.g. an accused can be charged 20 years after an act has occurred. The exception to this point is treason, which has a 3-year limitation period.
- Police require a warrant to arrest under an Indictable Offence (warrants are required to be signed by judge).
- Police only need to have reasonable and probable grounds to believe that the accused has committed the offence (as opposed to having directly witnessed the act as in a Summary Conviction offence).
- Accused does have to submit fingerprints when required to appear to answer to an indictable offence.
- Appeals always go to the Provincial Court of Appeal first, and then on to the Supreme Court of Canada.
- Accused convicted under an Indictable Offence can apply for pardon after 5 years.

Misdemeanour

The distinction between a felony and misdemeanour has been abolished by most other common law jurisdictions (e.g. Crimes Act 1958 (Vic., Australia) s. 332B(1), Crimes Act 1900 (NSW., Australia) s. 580E(1)).

Those jurisdictions have generally adopted some other classification, e.g. in Canada, Australia, the Republic of Ireland and the United Kingdom, **the crimes are divided into "Summary offences" and "Indictable offences"**

A misdemeanour in many common law legal systems, is a "lesser" criminal act. Misdemeanours are generally punished much less severely than felonies, but theoretically more so than administrative infraction (also known as regulatory offences).

Many misdemeanours are punished with monetary fines. Usually only repeat misdemeanour offenders are punished by actual jail time. It is highly unlikely that a first time misdemeanant will serve any jail time.

Allergies and Alerts:

Although, at the time of writing Food Allergen Labelling was not required by law. As of August 4, 2012 it is a requirement. Law or not, I suggest being pro-active and create customer awareness. It is prudent to advertise on the menu items which are commonly known as **allergens**. Care is to be taken for the not so obvious; hidden ingredients, like dried shrimp used to flavour Southeast Asian dishes, or unintentional garnishes like crushed walnuts atop a salad. Alternatively, a disclaimer stating that menu items may contain allergens could be sufficient, although it would necessitate conversation between guests and servers.

For a list of common allergens visit:
http://www.hc-sc.gc.ca/fn-an/securit/allerg/fa-aa/index-eng.php

Canada's new food allergen labeling regulations came into force on **August 4, 2012,** for Food Allergen Labelling Regulations visit:
http://www.hc-sc.gc.ca/fn-an/label-etiquet/allergen/index-eng.php

In addition to the required disclosure of allergens, consider to reveal other ingredients which could be harmful to Lactose intolerant, Celiac disease affected, and Diabetics customers. Obviously it is not necessary to identify that items made with milk or cream like a crème brulée contains milk or cream and eggs and sugar, but often milk-powder is added to baked goods or sauces and should be disclosed. Oriental food items often contain a large amount of sugar and could be harmful to a diabetic.

A Canadian book I would wholeheartedly recommend is: Canadian Hospitality Law, Liabilities and Risks, Current Edition, by Donald Longchamps and Bradley H. Wright, published by Nelson Education Ltd. @ 2007—ISBN: 0-17-640721-9

Service Standards, Methods, and Styles

Chapter 8

Now that the menu has been perfected,
how is it presented and
served to the guests?

Contributed by Jeannine L. Pharand-Theyer,
Professor, George Brown College, Toronto, Ontario, Canada.

To make the best meal or the most exotic drink memorable, it must meet the expectation of the customer's palate as well as the expectations inherent in excellent customer service.

The goal is to make every customer contact within the establishment an event. In general, people remember individual highlights of an event or a meal, but to make the entire event memorable, all components of the event must harmonize.

The location, the decor, how guests are greeted, the table settings, the taste and presentation of food and beverage, and the style of service used must be complemented in equal measures by service excellence in the attentiveness of staff, the presentation of the bill, and the last contact that demonstrates genuine appreciation for this guest interaction.

Best practices in service standards require all employees who have direct contact with customers to fulfill a well-defined role. Respective duties and responsibilities must clearly be understood by all stakeholders within the establishment, from the line employees to supervising managers. Depending on the particular establishment, this required knowledge could come either from previous industry experience or from training.

Specifically, all employees who have direct contact with customers, or who are involved in the sale of catered affairs and banquets and preparation or service of food and beverage need to be knowledgeable about the establishments **specific service standards and service styles.** Establishments that support this model may provide a manual identifying their specific standards and procedures.

> *Service styles and service methods are not the same thing.*
>
> *A service method dictates the organization of a meal. Service styles can combine several methods of service*

Service Styles, Formal and Informal

- American (Plate)—informal or formal
- Buffet or Self-Service—informal
- Cafeteria or Counter style—informal
- English or Family Style (Platter)—informal
- French (Guéridon)—formal
- Russian (Escoffier dishes, platters)—formal
- Room (In-room dining)—service style is depending on establishment
- Butler (Reception)—formal or informal

"Classical" Service Staff Identification, in French and English

Maître d'hôtel, Directeur (Chef) de restaurant	Director of Service/Manager
Sommelier	Wine Steward
Hôte or hôtesse	Host/Hostess
Captain	Head Server—Front Waiter
Chef du rang	Server—Back Waiter
Commis de rang	Busperson
Maître fromager - Affineur	Cheese specialist

BREAKFAST	LUNCH	DINNER
Table décor (flowers—fresh fruit basket—newspaper)	**Table décor** (flowers—centre pieces, neutral fragrance)	**Table décor** (candles, flowers, centre pieces, neutral fragrance)
Juices, coffee and/or tea	Appetizer	Appetizer
Continental	Soup	Soup
English	Salad	Sorbet or Salad
European, Cold meats & Cheeses	Entrée, Alternative meals	Entrée, Alternative meals
Alternative meals	Dessert	Salad
	Coffee and/or Tea	Cheese
		Dessert
		Coffer and/or Tea
		Friandises / Mignardises

Setting a table appropriately for the applicable meal period

The appearance of the "set table" is directly influenced by the type and style of menu and the style of service.

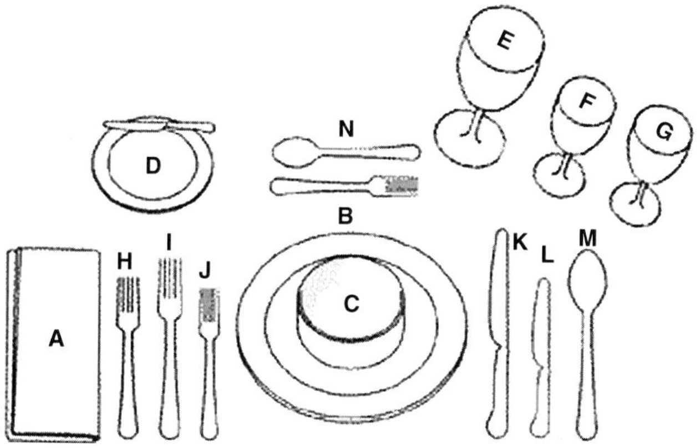

A	B	C	D	E
Serviette (napkin)	Service plate	Soup bowl on plate	Bread & butter plate with butter knife	Water glass
F	**G**	**H**	**I**	**J**
White wine	Red wine	Fish/Appetizer fork	Dinner fork	Salad fork
K	**L**	**M**	**N**	
Service knife	Fish knife	Soup spoon	Dessert spoon and cake fork	

Standard banquet table settings

Illustration sourced from http://didyouknow.org/tablesettings

In the above illustrated standard banquet table setting, the salad fork was placed to be used after the main course. However, it is more commonly located between "H, Fish or Appetizer fork" and "I, Dinner fork." Note that it often is recommended that the salad fork (J) is placed to the left of the dinner fork (I). In today's service style, cutlery is placed in the sequence of consumption of the various courses, starting from both sides, progressing toward the plate. If the menu consists of more than three courses, additional cutlery would be added (or replaced) as needed.

Note to Table Settings

Flatware is another word for cutlery. The knife was the first piece of metal cutlery, traced back to as early as 2000 BCE, spoons to about 5000 BCE, and the earliest ones were made of stone or clay. Forks first appeared about the 9th century, whereas chopsticks were already used in China during the Shang dynasty in 1766-1122 BCE.

Service Methods

1) Table d'hôte
- Service of the same menu items at an established set price to all guests.
- Guests do not have to belong to the same group.

2) Banquet
- A predetermined number of affiliated guests are served the same set, or table d'hôte menu at the same time.
- Menu items and beverages are predetermined by the host/organizer.

3) À la Carte
- Each guest chooses his or her meal from menu selections.
- Each meal is priced separately.

4) Reception

Butler service: Each guest helps him- or herself to bite-sized food items (amuse-bouche and/or hors d'oeuvres) and beverages carried around by the wait staff on trays or available from the bar.

Dining Room and Beverage Management Service Styles

Note: The following listing of service styles is based on my personal experience and research. Subsequently, I modified what I have written and published previously to conform to today's industry standards. Every sector of our industry is constantly looking to improve efficiency, safety, and guests' comfort. In the guest service area, front of the house, important changes were made to the method of service, and subsequently to the historical styles. In the past, based on respect and tradition the eldest female at a table was served first—nowadays, to avoid the stigma of identifying a particular age group, a table and seat/chair numbering system has been established and whichever seat/chair is identified as seat 1 (one) will be served first. Perhaps the most important change occurred in plate service: Where in the past plates were served from the left and cleared from the right, in the current method, plates are served from the right and cleared from the right.

The two most often incorrectly identified styles are Russian and French. Banquets almost always use Russian service style, but because this style uses silver platters and other silver utensils, it is often mistaken with French service.

French or Guéridon

- Preparing, cooking, assembling, and/or finishing food and/or beverage items in front of guests (salads, flambéed desserts, or specialty drinks).
- Food and/or beverages are partially prepped and brought to the table-side on a cart (guéridon)
- A guéridon has a cutting board and usually a small heating unit (réchaud) to help prepare the food.
- Chefs normally performed the cooking and received the title "chef de rang."
- Assistants known as commis de rang assist chef de rang, bring food, and clear plates.
- Chefs must be skilled to perform the table-side cooking under watchful eyes and must have excellent presentation skills as well.
- In the past it was considered a profession as this style became fashionable.

Rules

1. Hot food items are finished on réchaud.
2. Serving spoon and fork used to serve (one utensil in each hand).
3. Everything served from right side with right hand.
4. Everything cleared from right side with right hand.
5. Servers work clockwise around table.

Advantages

- High degree of attention to guests.
- Leisurely service (entertainment and showmanship).

Disadvantages

- Staff must always be showcasing (attitude, pressure).
- Inconsistency of food preparation among chefs and service staff.
- Ventilation of restaurant (flambé is a potential fire hazard) necessary.
- Using guéridons limits the numbers of tables in the restaurant due to extra space requirements.
- Table side (show) equipment is expensive.
- Longer service times (lower table turnover).
- High cost (occupancy) per diner.

Common ratio: 2 Servers for 2 tables (8 or 10) in teams of two.

Another type of guéridon service is the Grill Room Service: The meat to be cooked is shown to the customer in the raw, and after a selection was made, it is cooked in view of the customer, either on a guéridon or on another portable cooking device like a raclette stove. The side dishes are prepared in the kitchen and come preplated.

Russian (Silver or Platter Service)

- All food is cooked and portioned in kitchen away from guests.
- All food is presented to guests on silver trays (Escoffier dishes and platters).
- Waitstaff serve food to guest from trays.

Rules

1. Serving spoon and fork used for service.
2. One platter per course of meal (holds all items needed for course)
3. Serve from left side of guest with right hand. Left hand balances platter; server moves counter-clockwise around table.

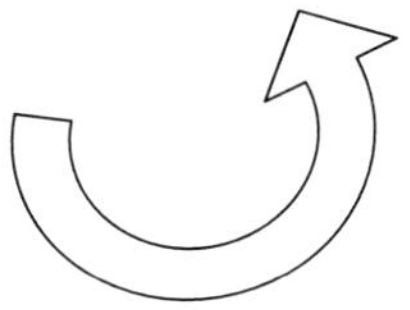

4. Platter held along left forearm and hand.
5. Separate spoon for sauce.
6. Separate utensils per course.
7. Sauce on platter is positioned farthest away from server, closest to guest plate.
8. Clear plates with right hand from right side in clockwise direction around table.
9. If serving hot courses, hot plates must be set in front of guest.
10. Plates placed just before platters brought from kitchen.
11. Service starts from lady on host's right or with eldest lady at table (traditional).

11 a. Service starts with seat number #1; usually seat #1 is the one closest to a door.

12. All children are served first.

Advantages

- Impressive style of service especially when cloches are being used.
- Less floor space needed than French style.
- Quicker than French service.
- Lower skill level than French service is required.
- Good quality control with appropriate portioning.

Disadvantages

- Learned skill needed to serve from platter, unlike plate service.
- Tables positioned to ease service.
- Food may not be very hot for last ones served.
- Individual portion size is limited by available quantity.
- Cost of equipment (platters, cloches, sauce-boat, silver cutlery for plating).
- Last person served may look at an unappealing platter.

Common ratio: 2 servers for 4 tables (8 or 10) or 1 server per 16 guests.

American Style (Plate)

- Portioning, plating, and garnishing done in kitchen.
- Service staff picks up food and serves it directly to guest.
- Food served from person's right with right hand.
- Removal of plates from right side with right hand.

Rules

1. Plated food served from right side with right hand, counter-clockwise around table while serving (after cloche—cover has been removed).
2. Clear plates with right hand from right side (stack on left hand), clockwise around table while clearing.
3. Clear smaller items (bread and butter plate, side dishes, utensils) to right of guest with right hand after entrée has been removed.

4. Serve beverages from right side using right hand moving in a clockwise direction around table (soup is considered a beverage).
5. Never reach across guest.
6. Stack plates as quietly as possible out of vision (scrape only enough off plates to stack).
7. Serve all at same time, clear all at same time.
8. Server should be discreet so that guest will not notice waitstaff.

Advantages

- Uncomplicated to teach and learn.
- Economical cost of equipment.
- Allows for fast service.
- Professional presentation since prepared in kitchen.
- Quality and quantity control since prepared in kitchen.
- Less space needed per guest (increased seating).

Disadvantages

- Not an elaborate service, therefore limited interaction with guest.

Common ratio: 2 servers for 4 tables (8 or 10) or 1 server per 16 guests.

Banquet Service

- All food preselected by host before arrival.
- All equipment necessary should be on table for guest to ease service.
- Decor, cutlery, glasses, and salt and pepper are preset.

Common ratio: 2 servers for 4 tables (8 or 10) or 1 server per 16 guests.

Buffet Service

Guests pick up part or all of their meal from displays in the dining room.

Buffet
- Guests pick up all food and beverages.
- Server only cleans up used dishes, glassware. and cutlery.

Modified Deluxe Buffet
- Tables are preset with utensils.
- Guests will be served beverages and dessert by staff.

Deluxe Buffet
- Some of the courses are served.
- Main entrée is chosen from buffet.
- Server clears between courses (before guest returns).
- Must have new plates for guests each time.

Rules

All displayed products must be labeled for proper identification.

Advantages

- Very easy to operate.
- Minimal staff training required.
- Lower staffing levels are needed.
- Higher guest satisfaction (choice of items and quantities they want).

Disadvantages

- Sanitation concerns (guest handling food).
- Amount of food needed, used, and wasted.
- Equipment expense (specialized pieces).
- Physical demand on guest; distance maybe challenging for handicapped guests (distances - wheelchairs)
- Guests having to wait in line.
- Allergy concerns.

Common ratio: 2 servers for 6 tables (8 or 10) or 1 server per 20 guests (covers).

Side Table Service (British)

- Hot plates placed on side table.
- Food presented on trays arranged in kitchen.
- Trays kept hot on réchaud (hotplate).
- Server or head of table builds plate and passes plate to waiting patrons.

Advantages

- Elegant presentation style.
- Allows for interaction between host and guest.
- Allows guests to select from offerings.
- Moderate skill level needed for servers.

Disadvantages

- Slower than American-style service.
- Smaller portions require extra plates being prepared.
- Equipment investment (cart, réchaud, platters).
- Staff training.
- Physical space needed for service.

Common ratio: 2 servers for 2 tables (8 or 10) in teams of two.

Butler Service (English Style)

- Combination of Russian (platters) and family style (help yourself).
- Food is brought fully prepared, on trays with handles from the kitchen.
- Trays held by butler to left side of the guest, allowing guests to serve themselves at table side using tray utensils.

Rules

1. Appropriately tempered plates preset on table.
2. Plates served from right side of guest with right hand, clockwise around table.
3. Butlers approach from left side holding tray level one inch (2½ to 3 CM) above rim of guest's plate.
4. Serving utensils on tray for guest, gravy boats.
5. Guests serve themselves using utensils and replace utensils for next person.
6. Butler moves counter clockwise around table.
7. Women and children are served first

Common ratio: 2 servers for 2 tables (8 or 10) in teams of two.

Family Style

- Bowls or platters placed on table; guests serve themselves.
- Various combinations of method (serve all courses or parts of courses).
- Very popular style in Oriental, ethnic, and themed restaurants.

Common ratio: 1 Server per 20 covers (guests).

Fast Food, Counter Service

Limited menu; customer can be served quickly.

- Items served on tray and customer moves to next station (cafeteria) or to table.
- Service is not a priority; the number of people served per hour is important.
- Efficiency is main concern; well-trained cash register (POS, point of sales system) operators are essential.

Common ratio: Depending on length of counter line and number of offerings, 1 to 2 servers (cashier may be required).

Room Service or In-room Dining

- All food and beverages is assembled by the kitchen (usually plated, but may also be arranged on platters) and brought to its destination by room-service personnel.
- Room service or in-room dining may also utilize the more elegant French service style.

Common ratio: 1 Server per room (1 for food and beverage).

Reception or "Flying" Service

- Food (hot or cold) and/or beverages brought around by servers.
- Modern reception service may offer food and beverage stations.

Common ratio: One server for 50 guests (one for food and one for beverage).

Common Clearing Procedures

See corresponding details listed at each service style. General rules: (1) Clear from right; (2) carry maximum of four plates at a time; (3) no scraping of plates at the table.

Clearing of trays should be done at side stations and/or back corridor.

Plates, glassware, and dishes are cleared from right, clockwise.

Front of the House "Mise en Place"

Everything set up in place:

The tables should be checked for level and balance—no wobble.

Chairs (especially aged wooden chairs) should be checked for soundness of construction, for wobble and appearance. Trendy chairs, like the transparent acrylic chairs, should be checked for cracks and scratches.

Tablecloths should be hanging at equal length around and/or over all sides of the table.

The silver (cutlery) should be placed 1 to 1½ inches (2½ to 4 CM) from the edge of the table.

A maximum of three pieces of silverware on each side of the plate (or its location if not set in) and two on top of the place setting. If more than three courses are being served, the required cutlery should be brought in for each course following.

Silver (cutlery in general) should be handled only by the handles and be polished.

Show plates should be spaced equally.

Number stands, flowers, candles and other arrangements, butter and margarine dishes, bread baskets, and filled salt and pepper shakers should be placed at the same spot on each table.

Contrary to the illustrated table setting, some establishments prefer to set the bread and butter plates 1 to 1½ inches (2½ to 4 CM) from the edge of the table in order for the napkin fold to fall flush with the table edge.

Water glasses are placed at right of dinner plate at the tip of the dinner knife.

Glassware is to be handled by the stem only. Ensure everything is polished.

Many books have been written about service; my favourite book is *At Your Service*, by John W. Fisher, The Culinary Institute of America, published by Wiley, ISBN 0-7645-5747-5

Jeannine L. Pharand-Theyer, Professor, George Brown College, Toronto, Ontario, Canada.

What do you get when you combine more than three decades of hotel catering, food and beverage, and high-end event management with boundless generosity and a drive to maintain the highest standards in everything you do?

Courtesy of Jeannine L. Pharand-Theyer, used with permission.

You get a first-rate educator who is respected by colleagues and students alike. That is Jeannine. Her illustrious career began at the Le Chateau Champlain (CP Hotels) in Montreal, Quebec, as the Restaurant Reservation Supervisor. In 1976 she was part of the team which opened the Meridien hotel in Montreal, Quebec discovering her passion for the world of catering.

In 1980 Jeannine then joined the Four Seasons Hotel Toronto before becoming the Assistant Food and Beverage Director at the Sutton Place Hotel. During this time, food production and deployment became the forefront of her training—training that served Jeannine well when she returned to the Four Seasons in 1989. Her career flourished here as she assisted the Food and Beverage Director with daily operations, establishing Corporate Food and Beverage Service standards, and managing all large Ballroom functions for a variety of clientele including Elton John, Michael Jackson, the Baroness of Rothschild, and Stevie Wonder.

Jeannine is a proud member of the National Association of Catering Executives (NACE) and a contributor for Operation Herbie, a fundraising initiative benefiting the Hospital for Sick Children. In 2007 Jeannine won the George Brown College Achievement award for Student Service Excellence. She has been a prominent figure in the catering industry for over 30 years, and her clients, colleagues, and students value her as an accomplished professional.

My favourite service utensils from the past: Escoffier Dishes

Courtesy of the author.

In addition to the "Service Standards, Methods, and Styles" it is important to emphasize information about the foremost money makers in food service; Banquets and Buffets.

Although the method and styles of banquets and buffets have been described in the preceding pages, the set-up considerations for such functions warrant further explanation.

Banquets:

Most of the arrangements for space, physical requirements like head-table, dance floor, AV–audio/visual needs, décor and ambiance, program of event, food to be served, the number of courses and sequence, the service style, the bar set-up and beverages to be served are made between the guests, the sales or catering staff. The chef maybe called upon to make menu suggestions over and above the pre-prepared banquet menus.

Buffets:

Buffets are either set-up as service style alternative to table service in a foodservice establishment open to the public, or, as an alternative and/or complementary to the traditional Russian or French service of a banquet.

The Chef in conjunction with the dining room manager in a foodservice establishment open to the public, or together with the catering/sales and banquet manager of the hotel or banquet venue decides on the theme and the type of food to be served and on the layout of the buffet table(s) and/or stations.

A banquet or buffet set-up is only limited by the clients imagination and budget and by the venues available space to accommodate the number of expected guests.

However, if the budget is not unlimited, there are industry standards to be considered:

Most of these standards are dictated by available furniture and equipment, which were developed to be functional and complementary to each other.

These standards were developed well before Canada converted to metric measurements and subsequently floor plans, tables, chairs, equipment and table-ware sizes are still expressed in inches and feet instead of centimetres and metres . . .

In room setup styles:

- Rounds
- Conference or Boardroom
- Classroom
- U-shape
- Hollow square
- Crescent rounds, buzz style or half-moon seating
- Theatre or auditorium
- Reception

Each of these styles has unique space and setup requirements.

Rounds are commonly set-up for meal periods and break-out discussions and are available in the following sizes (measured by diameter)

24″ (61 cm) seats 2-3 people, most common in bar height 42″ (107 cm) referred to as high-boy or cruiser tables.
36″ (91.5 cm) seats 4-6 people, can be at dining 30″ (76 cm) or bar height
48″ (122 cm) seats 6 persons
54″ (137 cm) seats 7 persons
60″ (152.5 cm) seats 8 people
66″ (168 cm) seats 10 people
72″ (183 cm) seats 10 -12 (accommodates up-to13)

Most common sizes are 36″ rounds (also called cocktail rounds) and 66″ rounds

Adding to the circumference of the table are chairs. Allow an additional 2′ (24″ or 61 cm) for a chair, as well as a minimum of 2′ (24″ or 61 cm) space for the service staff to maneuver around. In summary, there needs to be at least a distance of 6′ (72″ 183 cm) from the edge and between each table.

Linen size to cover a round table to the floor is measured by adding together the diameter and twice the height of the table.

A 60″ round which is 30″ high would need a tablecloth of 120″ (60 widths + 30 heights x 2) It is important that tables are placed in straight rows to create symmetry.

Conference or Boardroom; If an actual boardroom table is not available it can be created by abutting two 6′ or 8′ x 30″ buffet tables. They are most commonly used for smaller groups of 15 to 20 people. They are excellent for interactive sessions.

Classroom or schoolroom setup, features rows of tables with chairs and is most often used for larger groups with presenters and/or AV (audio-visual) presentations. Classroom tables are 18″ (46 cm) wide and 4′, 6′ or 8′ long.

U-shape and Hollow-square are perfect setups for larger working groups of 20 to 40 people allowing for each of them to be easily seen and heard, offers work-space for note-taking and digital devices. A u-shape setup also allows for presenters and/or AV presentations.

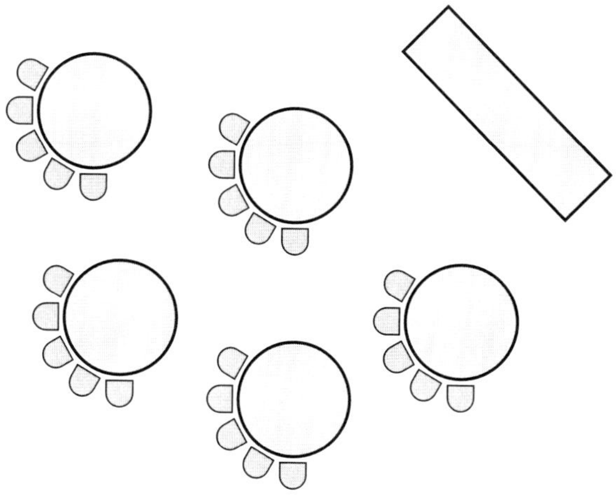

Crescent rounds are round tables with the surrounding chairs placed in a crescent or half-round arrangement. This potentially formal theatre style setup is facing a speaker, lectern/podium or AV and is ideal for a discussion or work group following a presentation.

Theatre or Auditorium other than an actual theatre or auditorium (lecture hall) setup refers to a room-setup with rows of chairs facing presentation. Ideally used for large groups. Not suitable for an extended period of time.

Emphasis is on allowing enough space between chair-rows, leaving enough room for people to easily and quickly get in and out of each row. There should be no more than fourteen chairs placed adjacent to each other without an aisle, and there should be a cross-aisle every tenth row.

Receptions often precede dinner functions and are meant for guest to mix and mingle. Finger food and liquid refreshments being served Butler style to standing guests and setups include high-boy or cruiser tables strategically placed throughout the reception room, as well as buffet tables for food and bar service. Approximately 6 to 7 square feet (0.6 to 0.65 square meters) floor space, per person, is needed, or it will be too crowded for comfort. Seating should be available for 20 to 25% of guests.

Tables; foodservice tables are commonly Rounds, Squares, Rectangles, Rounded ends (two half rounds abutted to a square or rectangle table) Ovals (Boardrooms), Communal (Long row). Each of them serves a different purpose or application.

Round tables are most often used and commonly are set-up for, six, eight, ten or twelve people to encourage conversations and for everyone to be equally well seen and heard.

Round table for 10

Oval or rounded tables

Classroom or communal table

Rectangle or boardroom table

It is not coincidental that a standard buffet table is 30 inches (76.2 cm) deep and 6 feet (183 cm) or 8 (244 cm) feet long, and a standard full-size chafing dish measures 14 x 25 inches (35.6 x 63.5 cm), allowing room for a small plate for utensils to be set affront a chafing dish.

The 30 inch depth of the table can accommodate buffet platters lengthwise or sideways as needed and up to three rows of 8 inch (20.3 cm), and two rows of 12 inch (30.5 cm) plates with room between them for comfortable handling by guests.

Buffet set-up considerations:

Buffets can be arranged in any line shape as long as they remain easily accessible and encourage quick customer flow. Ideally, a buffet should be fully or at least partially staffed to assist customers in making a choice and help them portioning food onto their plates, as well as for

Actual Boardroom table

Oval Banquet table

Classic reception set-up

Theatre style set-up

portion cost control. Carving stations should be in the centre of double sided lines, or at the end of single lines. It is not uncommon to place carving or cooking stations in different areas of the room and have a line for common accompaniments. If staffing is not in the budget, small cards or label identifying individual dishes will help the customer making a choice. It is also advisable to post; clearly visible, ingredients used which are commonly known allergens. There should be a separate buffet line for every 50 customers. The start of the buffet line, single or dual should always be the plates, whereas cutlery, nicely bundled, should be at the end of the line, unless it is already set on the table.

For stand-up receptions 6″ (15 cm) plates are easier to handle then the common 9″ to 12″ (23 cm to 30 cm) plates.

Decoration with flowers, candles or ornaments, ice, fruit or vegetable carvings, should be in harmony with the theme of the function or buffet. Like a basket of root vegetable and ornamental pumpkins for Thanks-giving would be quite appropriate. It is often beneficial to use coloured tablecloth instead of white ones to drape the buffet line, since white ones will look less messy once they become stained with spilled food items.

Buffet set-ups

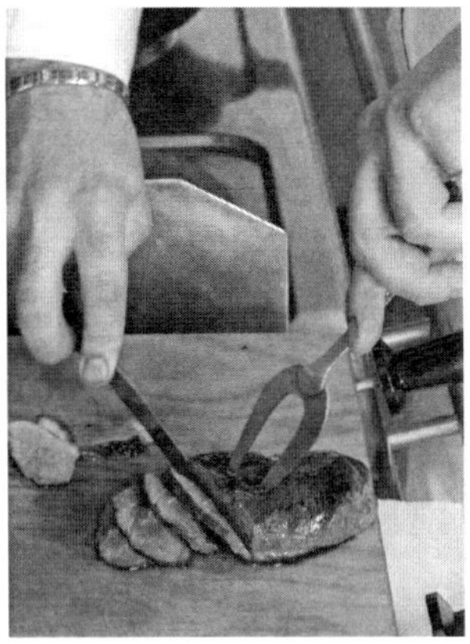

Dessert tables and hot beverage tables should be separate from the main buffet line. For smaller functions these two stations can be combined but usually it slows down the line-ups.

The flow from start to the end of the buffet line is ideally arranged, but not limited to the following sequence;

1. Plates,
2. Breads and butter/margarine
3. Appetizers and sandwiches
4. Salads and dressings
5. Cold condiments
6. Soups
7. Chafing dishes with pasta dishes
8. Chafing dishes with vegetables and starch accompaniments
9. Chafing dishes for hot food main courses (all food items should be cut into easy to handle portions with the most expensive food items in the last chafing dishes, or at the carving station)
10. Carving station
11. Condiments for carved food items
12. Cutlery, if not already set at the table

I recommend using half size chafing inserts, since they are easy to refill and never appear too empty, it also discourages most customers from over-filling their plates feeling obliged to leave something for the next person.

Stations and themed stations: are usually placed away from the main buffet line to divert traffic and to add interest. These stations are often equipped with cooking equipment handling one or two different items, or are simply carving stations with different types of products.

As previously mentioned, the buffet line itself, or stations, can be arranged in any shape desired; from straight tables, to U-shape, S-shapes, triangular shapes as long as it is done with the customer in mind.

A few basic buffet table arrangements

Appendix: Chef's Interviews and Contributions

Chapter 9

Norm Myshok, CCC

Norm Myshok CCC, is past Chairman of the Canadian Culinary Institute, the education arm of the Canadian Culinary Federation.

In my role as Corporate Chef for a food manufacturer I deal with a wide range of foodservice operations. From small franchised "grab and go" food kiosks to business, industry, and educational institute caterers to 3000 outlet franchised chains, my customers are all looking for the same solutions, i.e., menu ideas that fit their concept or brand, deliver the desired financial performance, and please their patrons.

While operational parameters, such as skill levels, style of service, and demographics, may differ, the recurring themes in the requests are very similar. The concept has to

- be executable by the line worker at the peak volume of business.
- utilize existing inventory as much as possible.
- be creative and have "cravability."

While at times this seems like a tall order, the process begins with researching the existing menu and facility setup. No matter how good a concept is, how economical the ingredients are, or how good the profitability of the menu item is, *if it doesn't fit operationally, it won't move forward from the concept stage.*

During the concept stage factors considered are

- current trends and how they relate to the operation. Not all operations want to be on the cutting edge. Depending on their market demographics some will be "close followers," some "rapid adapters," others simply want a revitalization of menu items or an extension of offerings that their patrons are seeking.
- availability of products. Large national chain operations need to know that all their outlets can get the identical product easily from their broad line distributor from coast to coast. Smaller, regional chains take a similar position but may want to be able to feature regional or local products on their menus. Independent operators may want to consider menu items that are sustainable and are prepared to use a variety of suppliers to achieve this goal. While sustainability and using local products are noble goals, it's not always possible. One of the key points for a successful operation is consistency—of product, of service, of quality and availability. Customers demand it and have a right to expect it. In terms of practicality, the best advice is "think globally, buy regionally, cook seasonally."

- ease of consistent execution at peak levels of business.
- cross-utilization of new products introduced and existing inventory.
- asking if the menu item fits within the financial parameters of the operation. That is to say, Will the selling price and food cost be in line with the budgeted values?

If you are the *chef patron* of the operation, you can put anything you wish on your menu. However, most chefs need to write, present, and defend new menus or items to CEOs, restaurant owners, marketing departments, or Food and Beverage Managers. As a menu concept moves from ideation into the validation stage, generally a test tasting by all parties brings forth the first objections or road blocks. At this point I like to ask four very penetrating questions.

1. Does the menu or menu item fit the concept or brand of the operation?

   There are times when the owner, marketing department, or F&B manager will walk into your office and state "you'll never guess what I saw in…." or " so and so has a Tex-Mex eggroll on the menu and it's selling like hotcakes and I would like to have the same item on the operations menu." If the food item doesn't fit the concept of your operation, the likelihood of its being a successful seller is greatly reduced.
2. Is this the best way to increase revenues and profitability?

   Developing successful menu items or new menus is a costly process. Mistakes are even costlier. Changes that you make on your menu affect overall menu and operational performance. Highly popular new menu items may not attract new customers or encourage the regulars to come more often. They may only cannibalize another menu items or even raise food and inventory costs if other items aren't selling and loss through spoilage occurs.
3. In this case, whose need is being filled?
4. Can I explain this to a four year old?

Domenic Chiaromonte

Photo courtesty of Dominic Chiaromonte.

Domenic Chiaromonte is the Executive Chef/Co-owner of T2 Restaurant just north of Toronto, as well as being a cookbook author, popular television chef, and catering industry consultant. Domenic began his chef apprenticeship while in his early twenties.

One of his earliest and most significant experiences was in Tokyo, where he first developed an appreciation for Eastern cuisine and styles of presentation, which continue to inform his work until this day.

On return from the East, his insatiable appetite for learning and the respect for food and culture took him to the Hilton Hotel Toronto to work under his greatest mentor, Albert Schnell. Chef Domenic has also worked side by side with many culinary superstars, such as Oprah's own chef Art Smith, and has apprenticed at Charlie Trotters in Chicago.

This on-the-job training combined with his formal Humber College education provided the platform for Domenic to quickly become an award-winning chef and plating champion. At the 2005 International Caterers Association (ICA) CATIEs (Catered Arts through Innovative Excellence), Domenic was awarded the prestigious first place award for Best Plate Presentation and Best New Food Trend.

He has also been featured on Food Network's *Superstar Chef Challenge*, Slice Network, Life Network, HGTV, Breakfast Television, CBS, and Fox Network in California as well as recently on *The CBS Early Show* live from New York City and Martha Stewart Radio. He has recently released his own book, *Creating the Unexpected*, and has just finished production of his very own TV series *My Favourite Dish"*.

While traveling the globe introducing himself to the cuisines of India, Morocco, Spain, Greece, Italy, Thailand, Japan, and China, Domenic has created his own distinct style, which he calls "Modern Canadian." Canada's melting pot of cultures has served as a personal canvas for his dishes and plating style. He has not only developed mastery for creating edible works of art, but he also transforms a gourmet dish into an extraordinary event.

Domenic, along with many news publications he contributed to *INSIDE the RECIPE BOX of the Catering Chef*, ISBN 13: 978-0-9802439-1-8 and wrote *Creating the Unexpected*. The books are available at T2 restaurant and online at Catersource.com.

About T2 lounge (Tazza 2):

177 Whitmore Road, Woodbridge, Ontario, Telephone: 905-850-9990

www.t2lounge.com/index.htm

Music lovers and food enthusiasts make T2 Lounge the popular destination for a great night out with sophistication, style, and a mature crowd. We welcome you for any special occasion event or just a special night out with friends.

Facility capacity: 80-seat restaurant, 70-seat banquet room, plus a 40-seat banquet room on the second floor. The new patio features 80 seats.

Interview

Q: What are your favourite menu creations?

A: When I do demo-cooking at the LCBO Summerhill location, the open-minded clientele is fabulous to demo for at these events.

Q: Domenic, I have seen demonstrating molecular cuisine in Canada and in Las Vegas. What future do you see for molecular cuisine?
A: I am really glad to be involved in molecular cuisine and the science knowledge I have gathered because of this involvement, but admittedly, I missed the hands-on traditional cuisine. Offering molecular cuisine outside of dedicated settings, you are as good as this new fad is understood, very instable—most people cannot relate. It also involves quite elaborate and expensive equipment and ingredients, and it is time-consuming in pre-preparation.

With the revamping of the restaurant I now take more time back in the kitchen, which I enjoy very much. We now also make our own bread and pastries.

Q: On average, how many meals are produced daily?
A: The restaurant is open for lunch and dinner Mondays to Saturdays. The weekly average is about 400, plus banquets and on-location caterings for about 200.

Q: The brigade, key positions, and hierarchy for all the properties you oversee?
A: Twelve persons working in the kitchen, including pastries, over two shifts, myself, two sous chefs, and trainee students from Woodbridge College.

I enjoy training aspiring young cooks who would like to get a taste for this rewarding career. During the interview I look mainly for one thing: passion—which is what I expect from every employee.

Q: What supporting departments are available to you?
A: Food is ordered by chef and sous chefs; the manager does the beverage ordering.

Purchasing is split between several suppliers. One-stop supplier Cisco is one of them; however, close-by a new place near here offers cash and carry and a recent price comparison showed up to 20 percent savings on a large number of items. The product is not delivered.

Kitchen staff management including hiring is done by Domenic.

Partner takes care of front of the house. He is also a chef by trade.

Q: Approximately how many different products you need to have in inventory to produce offered menu items?
A: Now that we are doing our own baked products the inventoried items increased to approximately 400.

Q: When you design, write or rewrite menus, do you put emphasis on cross utilisation?
A: Because we are a fairly small operation with limited space, cross utilisation is vital to our operation.

Q: What are your thoughts when you create new menu items?
A: My thoughts are on my clients. They have become a lot more sophisticated because they travel and watch various food shows. I need to create something that they can replicate at home, yet something they would normally not cook themselves. Menus are changed four times a year and we create daily specials.

Q: With your product needs, can you incorporate the 100-mile rule of purchasing and are you concerned about the carbon footprint?
A: In the summer we really try, but in the winter it does not make much sense. Canada cannot produce many of the products a foodservice establishment needs. We try to by local as much as possible to make some impact on carbon print of shipping products.

Q: How do you deal with dead stock?
A: Because we emphasize cross utilisation we don't have to deal a lot with dead stock, but if we do end up with some, we do "family dinners" we invite the family of a staff member and utilize the products cooking for them.

Q: How do you manage purchasing considerations and control?
A: We use a par stock list for staples; for other menu items, since we change the menu frequently, we do daily specials and have catering and banquets. We purchase what and when we need it. Besides the staple products, we hardly have enough products in inventory to be controlled.

Q: What are your thoughts during the process of creating new (other than seasonal) menu items and in what way do you consider your customers while creating a menu item description?
A: I do a lot of Internet research for product knowledge. Whenever we see something new and exciting, we ask ourselves "Will those work with our demographic clientele?"

The next thought is our unique style of presentation to the client. Most of the time we do not use traditional plates—instead we use rectangular stone tiles—how will this impact on our service staff?

Another important thought on our mind is, What if does not sell? Our menu offerings must either blend in or stand out from what our clientele expects from our restaurant. We often test new product ideas in banquets or special events since it provides almost instant feedback from numerous people. One must also keep in mind that the available staff in this area is not the same calibre of trained career staff accessible to downtown operations. Therefore, staff training to make them more knowledgeable is considerably more extensive and subsequently more costly.

Q: How do you plan for and maintain consistent plate presentation?
A: I believe that everything must be open to creativity—presentations can be different—as long as the taste is consistent. Sous chefs and cooks must follow recipes because our regular clientele expects consistency in taste. I keep my menu item description short and to the point and ensure that service staff to have a good knowledge of the menu to make recommendations.

Q: Do you adhere to a standard process (self-imposed or other) in creating a printable menu item description?
A: I write all menus myself, with input from the sous chefs. I use novel names to create excitement and innovation, which creates interaction with clients.

Q: Which method to calculate a menu selling price is your preferred method?
A: I still use the various methods I learned in school—I still have the textbook. Most of the time I use the ideal-cost method, but in some cases I resort to the prime-cost method if the labour might be equal or higher than the food cost. Being a restaurant in a local community, I also need to be sensitive to competitive establishments, although I may charge more than the competition if I use a high-end product. Our Black Angus steak will most likely be priced higher than a regular "AA" brand steak. Speaking of steaks, my preference is to use PEI cattle because the meat has a different characteristic than prairie cattle. I will record on the menu Black Angus steak and let the servers explain the difference. Menu descriptions need to be simple yet attractive to encourage server and customer interaction. Menus are no longer written the traditional way, the way I learned it. I often compare my writing to the writing of my mentor, Chef Albert Schnell.

Q: If your kitchen staff would ask you, What is a good food cost percentage for your type of establishment?, what would you tell them?
A: I would tell them that one needs to be concerned with making a profit. The best food cost may not be a substitute for profit margin. Catering and banquets can be better controlled, because the client will be paying for the labour and food based on the level of quality he desires.

Q: Do you have a need and demand to follow trends?
A: Absolutely. I always try to be innovative and to set trends. I am to some extent of a trend setter.

Q: What influences you when making a selection of tableware to complement the food presentation as well as the atmosphere of the establishment?
A: I like to use many different ways and utensils to present my food. The look has to be fresh and innovative. I rotate my presentations to keep them exciting and trendy. I look toward New York and Chicago for new ideas.

Q: How frequently do you monitor the performance of offered menu items and do you use specific method or software for it?
A: We recently switched to a Pixel Point POS—the built-in reports in this system generates allow us to analyse the sales mix. My partner does the reports. Pasta and pizza are the best sellers; meats, because of the high quality we are buying, are not as profitable.

Q: What is your perception of, and what do you expect from a "perfect menu"?
A: I should sell well and make the expected profit.

Q: Chef Domenic, for my final question I am asking you for any other thoughts you may have on menu planning for "today's customer that you would like to share with readers.
Product knowledge is the key. Many menus are too complex with eighteen items used in one dish. Sure, it sounds amazing but is a great challenge for the even best-trained taste buds. Reality is, if the composition is too complex, you really have no idea what you are eating. You need to be concerned how your body reacts to it. Ideally, after you have eaten, you should feel comfortably satisfied. You should feel content, not full, because what you eat weighs heavily in your stomach.

Q: I have one more question. From your personal experience with molecular cuisine, what do you feel is the future of molecular cuisine in Canada?
A: I would say the initial phase of innovation has slowed down. I don't think Toronto or other major cities in Canada can succeed offering only molecular cuisine. I predict that it will manifest itself as a novelty item for one or two courses, perhaps table-side prepared.

For Domenic's latest menu creations please visit:
www.t2lounge.com/menu.htm

Robert Bartley, Executive Chef

Photo courtesy of Robert Bartley.

Robert Bartley is Director of Culinary, Executive Chef, for the Air Canada Centre, the Air Canada Club, the Platinum Club, e11even, the Hot Stove Club, and the Real Sports Bar & Grill, Toronto, Ontario, Canada.

Air Canada Centre

The Air Canada Centre is considered to be the leader in the industry of stadium hospitality. We serve over 20,000 fans at any given event!! With over 75 menu items in our 26 concessions, 3 private clubs, 144 suites, and a fully operational catering company that can tailor any size of event, large or small, on our property or offsite.

Select from fresh-made fruit cups at Zielinski's Orchard, giant baked cookies at Sweet Wally's, Jamie Kennedy's seasoned fries, house smoked pulled pork sandwiches, or visit Burkie's Dog House for a customized hot dog prepared right in front of you. Our food and beverage team is committed to using only the highest quality ingredients available, paired with an award-winning wine cellar headed up by Canada's first and only female Master Sommelier.

Our kitchens at the Air Canada Centre are overflowing with a wide breadth of culinary talent that makes dining a unique and memorable culinary experience. With Director of Culinary Robert Bartley, one Executive Chef, and six Chef de Cuisines and Sous Chefs, we have the culinary experience and depth to deliver an exceptional gastronomic experience. From butter-basted lobster to bacon-wrapped hot dogs, our culinary umbrella is vast.

We have developed a network of purveyors that provide us with fresh fish, game, cheeses, meats, and vegetables from across Canada. We are dedicated to serving you only the finest ingredients and products available.

Not only do we prepare food for over 20,000 fans a game, but we are also responsible for providing our teams meals that are engineered for performance. We deliver the same quality to our teams and visiting teams as we do with our fans. Only the best for our best!

The food and beverage team is proudly fuelling our company's vision to WIN!

Platinum Club

Welcome to the Platinum Club. Our club features a stunning 3,000-bottle floor to ceiling Sterling Three Palms wine cellar that surrounds a marble tasting table. The room also includes two sub-zero fridges to keep white, dessert, and sparkling wines perfectly cared for and ready to serve. Opposite the wine cellar, the Krug Room is surrounded by glass for a more exclusive and intimate atmosphere. Both of these unique dining experiences can be booked through the Club Manager.

The Platinum Club at the Air Canada Centre provides the most luxurious dining experience in the city of Toronto. In collaboration with the Vice President of Food & Beverage Michael Doyle and the award-winning Fleur De Lis Design Team, the recently renovated restaurant now hosts 260 guests for business dinners, wine tastings, or a romantic evening for two.

Established in 1999, the restaurant provides Platinum seat holders with a sophisticated environment to enjoy exceptional food and premium service. The atmosphere includes soft lighting paired with rich colours and textures that are surrounded by elegant handmade décor crafted by various Canadian artists. Guests can enjoy their experience in one of our three unique dining spaces that come together to make the Platinum Club a destination. The Sterling Three Palms Merlot Wine Cellar is a glass-enclosed room surrounding an eight-person marble table, ideal for private dinners or wine tastings. Opposite the wine cellar stands the Champagne Room, an eight-person private dining experience featuring a mother of pearl wall and a solid mahogany and ebony table. Finally, our main dining areas are ideal for accommodating parties of any size for exceptional cuisine before the event or during intermission. Two beautiful onyx backlit bars are located on either side of the wine cellar. Both are perfect for a pregame or intermission cocktail.

Accompanying the extravagant décor, the revised menu created by our Executive Chef and Director of Culinary Robert Bartley will excite your appetite with an array of classic cuisine including Roasted Salmon, Herb & Pecan Crusted Rack of Lamb, complete with Chocolate Banana Cake and Mini Crème Brule. To complement the cuisine, our Head Sommelier, alongside her certified team, pair your food with our award-winning wine program of over 500 labels from various regions around the world.

The newly renovated club is overseen by Senior Management, one Executive Chef, and one Chef de Cuisine. For reservation inquiries, please dial 416-815-5983.

Please note it is suggested you allow a minimum of 1.5 hours to dine before each event.

If you have any special requests, or to decant your wine selection prior to arrival, please call the Platinum Club directly at 416-815-5984.

For inquiries about booking private functions or special events, please contact 416-815-5500 ext 5067.

Air Canada Club

In this upscale dining room you can enjoy great service, an outstanding selection of wine from the fully visible, glass-enclosed wine cellar with sommeliers to cater to your every need. With outstanding sightlines to the ice, court, or concert, the Air Canada Club boasts a sexy yet classy design of light oak tables and soft plush leather chairs. The bar is a must-see with its 75-foot backlit translucent onyx design that makes it one of the longest in the city. Unique to the club are the rail seats, which allow fans a great view of both concert and sporting events.

The menu offers a selection of sophisticated comfort foods including fan favourites: Red Wine Braised Veal Shank, Slow-cooked BBQ Baby Back Ribs, Roasted Mushroom Tagliatelle, and melt-in-your-mouth Prime Rib.

Air Canada Club surrounds you with photos of hockey and basketball greats as well as concert superstars. A 1,200-bottle wine cellar centered in the dining room adds both elegance and functionality while promoting the Wine Spectator award-winning wine list.

Soft lighting surrounds the long onyx bar while warm wood finishes complement the restaurant's focus on luxury and quality for our fans. Networking and interaction are key in this club, as is the ambiance.

Hot Stove Club

The Hot Stove Club, established in 1963, has a long-standing history with the Toronto Maple Leafs Hockey Club. Its original location on the grounds of Maple Leaf Gardens served as a great place for its members to dine and socialize before and after the game. The level of service and quality of food soon became legendary in the city of Toronto, serving its guests at the Gardens for over thirty years.

In 1999 Air Canada Centre opened as the new home of the Toronto Maple Leafs and Toronto Raptors. Back by popular demand, the Hot Stove Club reopened its doors at the Air Canada Centre to both old and new members. The classic décor incorporates rich wood, luxurious accents, and a personalized style of service. Crisp white linens drape the tables set with crystal stemware and an exceptional wine list to choose from. Meet friends in the bar area and enjoy our fine selection of cognac, scotch, or an ice-cold lager or ale while watching the game on Sony TVs in HD. Guests enjoy watching their meals being prepared in our open-concept kitchen.

Today, we still pride ourselves on providing the rich history that surrounds our past. Our Sous Chef invites you to enjoy our "Chop House" inspired menu and ambiance in the spirit of the Toronto Maple Leafs and Toronto Raptors and the love of the game. The Hot Stove is a great place for its members to enjoy a classic dining experience and catch up with old friends before, during, and after the game.

e11even

Welcome to our labour of love. To us, e11even is more than a restaurant. It's our home. Our own kitchen and dining room, opened to our guests, whom we consider it a privilege to entertain. We've put thought and care into everything from the simplest of ingredients to each place setting. e11even is the best of us. Welcome.

Sports Bar & Grill

If you're hungry, Tony Glitz knows how to cure what ails you. He's our Executive Chef and in-house super-fan,so he knows a thing or two about mixing fine cuisine with gritty cheer fests. You get fresh ingredients cooked from scratch (no frozen chicken wings here) and intense variety—from slow-roasted baby back ribs and hand-crafted burgers to hand-cut aged Canadian beef and fresh cut fries. Tony also threw in some culinary flair with flavours that span East Asia, the Caribbean, Latin America, and Europe. Let's talk about chicken wings again…with over eleven types on the menu, there's a wing for everyone, but you have to try Chef Tony's Thai Chicken wings… it's the recipe that got him the job…literally!

He's equal parts sports fan and kitchen wizard, which means that win or lose, Tony makes sure that all fans leave fulfilled.

Interview Questions and Answers

Q: On average, how many meals are produced daily?
A: I direct the food operations as a whole for Maple Leaf Sports and Entertainment (MLSE). This involves quick service (concessions), catering, private clubs, restaurants, suites, cafeteria, sports bar, and a casual upscale restaurant.

We run two stadiums, Air Canada Centre and (Bank of Montreal) BMO field as well as two restaurants, Real Sports Bar & Grill and e11even. During the hockey and basketball season, we serve 800 à la carte meals, 500 catered meals to media, players' wives, and board of directors, referees, alumni, and gondolas. We also operate 30 concessions that feed 18,500 people any given game night.

At Real Sports Bar & Grill (RSBG) we serve 500 to 600 à la carte lunches and over 2000 dinners. At e11even we serve average 300 people each day for both lunch and dinner.

Q: What is the structure and size of the brigade you oversee?
A: We have a Vice President of Food and Beverage, one Director of Culinary, 60 full-time Food and Beverage management, including a Director of Quick Service (QS) and RSBG operations. We have 4 Executive Chefs, 1 Executive Sous-Chef, 1 Pastry Chef, 3 Chefs de Cuisine, 5 Sous Chefs, and 30 Supervisors. A total of approximately 160 cooks in our Restaurant and Catering Division and 200 in QS.

Q: Approximately, how many different products do you need to have in inventory to produce offered menu items?
A: We have numerous products needed to run this facility. Close to 200 is my best estimate. We do use many core products many different ways, e.g., at RSBG we have six menu items all driven from one core product, chicken tenders, including an appetizer, entrée, salad, and sandwich. We rely on learned volumes from sales report. We understand our product mix very well, which allows us to accurately predict our sales and volumes of each core ingredient. In QS we rely on an inventory based ordering system—i.e. what gets sold gets purchased. We have many ways to use dead stock. We can utilize many proteins in our cafeteria and media catering and also contribute substantially to Second Harvest.

Q: When you design, write, or rewrite menus, do you put emphasis on cross utilisation?
A: Number 1: Any new menu item is created for our fans, not the chefs. We do numerous surveys, focus groups, one-on-ones with our fans to get their input on new menu items. Then we look to see if we can get quality ingredients, consistently. Then we look staffing and execution to be able to reproduce that menu on a consistent basis. Then we prepare these menus items for internal management to gain feedback on how to make them better. We will do the same with fans. Once these steps are completed, we then look at margin the item will deliver, and if it makes money, fans want and love it, we are able to produce consistently, only then we consider putting it on the menu.

Q: How do you accomplish purchasing of various products?
A: See above. By understanding who our customer is and catering accordingly.

Q. Do you adhere to a standard process (self-imposed or other) in creating a printable menu item description?
A. We have different philosophies on this, dependant on type of item and where it is for—i.e., in QS less is more. Highlighting with a quick slash attracts the customer and makes it easy for them to see and read—i.e., Cheeseburger, Foot Long Hot Dog.

In the restaurant you need to tell a quick story of what the customer is eating. My preference is NOT in fluff, nor just listing ingredients. The item description needs to be descriptive and enticing— i.e., at e11even, the Signature Roast Chicken/Mashed Potatoes/Country Stuffing.

Q: With your product needs, can you incorporate the 100-mile rule of purchasing and are you concerned about the carbon footprint?
A: It is important to keep current with trends. I believe in supporting local farmers but I will go outside of that to get ingredients our fans/customers want.

Q: Which method to calculate a menu selling price is your preferred method?
A: I prefer to understand not only the cost of the goods to purchase but also the labour cost to produce any menu item. We analyze gross margins on cost of goods sold (COGS) of goods and set a target for what we would like to achieve in a category. Some categories will have higher margins than others BUT when you put the sales in to a preference report the overall number is what we like to analyse, i.e., on a menu you may have steak and calamari (round number for

illustration purposes only). The steak (cost of goods) COG% will be higher than the calamari. Then we set a cost of labour (COL) to each to understand the total cost for that menu item.

If you compare a steak versus calamari, the steak's selling price is $50.00:

- Food and labour costs are $25.00
- Net profit is $25.00
- Food cost is 50%

Calamari's selling price is $12.00

- Food and labour cost is $3.00
- Net profit is $ 9.00
- Food cost is 25%

In this example, per cover I would rather sell more steaks than calamari even though the cost % is double it. It contributes more to the bottom line.

Q: If your staff would ask you, What in your opinions is a good food cost percentage for your type of establishment(s), what would you tell them?
A: Dependant on the type of facility, QS you should be able to get 25%. For restaurants, 30–33%

Q: Do you have a need and demand to follow trends?
A: Yes, 100%.

Q: What influences you when making a selection of tableware to complement the food presentation as well as the atmosphere of the establishment?
A: I consider all when introducing a menu item. What cutlery is needed, the look of the dish on the table alongside the candle, flower, wine glass, linen, etc

Q: How and how frequently do you monitor the performance of offered menu items, and do you use specific software for it?
A: We run P-mixes every month to identify what is working and what is not. We use our POS to deliver reports. Mostly Eatec, Aloha, and MenuLink.

Q: What is your perception of, and what do you expect from a "perfect menu"?
A: A perfect menu is a balance between giving your targeted customers what they want, what is profitable for the owner/operator, what provides employment opportunities and growth for the staff, and what is aligned with the vision of the restaurant.

Q: Are there any other thoughts you may have on menu planning for today's customer you would like to share with readers?
A: I think I have listed most of them but if nothing else, cook for the customer first—it's a win/win combination.

For the various menu offerings of the before mentioned locations please visit:
www.theaircanadacentre.com/restaurants/index.asp
www.theaircanadacentre.com/foodandbeverage/quickservice/InSeatMenu.asp
www.theaircanadacentre.com/restaurants/AirCanadaClub/LeafsMenu.asp
www.theaircanadacentre.com/restaurants/PlatinumClub/DinnerMenu.asp
www.theaircanadacentre.com/restaurants/HotStove/RaptorsMenu.asp
www.e11even.ca/menus

TONY FERNANDES

Photo courtesy of Tony Fernandes.

Tony Fernandes began manifesting his passion for food at age 11 when he learned to cook alongside his father, who was a cooking instructor at the Institute of Hotel Management in Mumbai, India.

Chef Tony later graduated from the same institute and began pursuing his culinary dreams.

To date, Chef Tony and his culinary teams have won forty medals from culinary competitions worldwide, including a Silver medal from the 2010 Culinary World Cup competition at Expogast, Luxembourg.

Chef Tony's infectious personality and culinary skill have garnered him coveted spots on Breakfast Television, *CBC News*, The Food Network's *I Do, Let's Eat*, Backyard Pleasures with Deborah Boland as well as recognition in dozens of hospitality print publications and *Resort to Cooking*, a cookbook featuring recipes by premier hotel chefs.

In addition to holding the position of Director of the Escoffier Society of Toronto, Chef Tony is an honorary lifetime member of the Emirates Culinary Guild in the capacity of Vice President, a member of the Les Toques Blanches and a Master Craftsman of the UK's Cookery and Food Association.

Known for his ability to fuse global flavours with top quality foods his guests know and love, Chef Tony is proud to be the Group Executive Chef and Food and Beverage Director for Royal Equator Inc, which owns and operates the Crowne Plaza Toronto Airport Hotel, the Four Points Sheraton Toronto Airport, and the Hilton Garden Inn Toronto/Mississauga.

Chef Tony began his professional training at the Taj Intercontinental Hotel Mumbai and went on to become the Executive Chef and Food & Beverage Director at some of the best five-star deluxe hotels in India, Saudi Arabia, and the United Arab Emirates. After moving his family to Canada in 2001, Chef Tony held the position of Executive Chef and Food & Beverage Director for The Hockley Valley Resort before moving to Royal Equator Inc.

In the winter of 2010, Chef Tony brought victory home from the prestigious Culinary World Cup competition in Expogast, Luxembourg. Chef Tony and his five team members competed against more than 2,400 chefs from 53 countries and won a silver medal for Canada based on their outstanding overall performance.

Chef Tony was also part of a team that is recognized in the *Guinness Book of World Records* for creating the Biggest Bowl of Biryani in the World—a feat that took place at the Heritage Village in Dubai in April 2001.

Chef Tony has personally catered to celebrities and prominent political figures, including various Hollywood and Bollywood stars, former Canadian Prime Minister Paul Martin, the president of India, the sheikhs of UAE, the first lady of Poland and international cricket teams.

Outside of the kitchen, Chef Tony is an accomplished musician, singer, and ballroom dancer.

Interview: On average, how many meals are produced daily?

A: 800 to 1200 depending on season.

Q: What is the structure of the brigade., and the key positions for all the properties you oversee?

A: One Executive Chef for all three properties, 2 Executive Chefs, 1 Executive Sous Chef, 1 Chef de partie, 36 Line Cooks, and 3 Prep Cooks.

Crowne Plaza Toronto Airport

www.cptayyz.com

Foodservice from 5:30 AM to 2 AM; Room Service: 24 hours
Banquet facility 12,000 square feet; 1 restaurant, La Brasserie, 140 seats; 1 piano bar & lounge, Rendezvous, 72 seats; Room service 489 rooms.

Hilton Garden Inn Toronto/Mississauga

www.torontomississauga.gardeninn.com

Foodservice available from 6 AM to 10 PM
Restaurant Great North American Grill & Bar, 55 seats; Pavilion Lounge bar, 80 seats; Room service for 154 rooms; 2500 sq ft combined banquet and meeting facilities.

Four Points by Sheraton Toronto Airport

http://www.fourpoints.com/torontoairport

Foodservice 6 AM to 1 AM
11,000 sq ft meeting and banquet facilities; De Maple restaurant, 100 seats; De Maple Lounge with 57 seats; and Room Service for 204 rooms.

Combined capacity:

Banquet facility: 25,500 sq ft meeting and banquet facilities, 3 restaurants: 285 seats, 3 bar/lounge: 129 seats and Room Service for 847 rooms.

Q: What supporting departments are available to you? i.e., Purchasing, Stewarding, Food & Beverage Control, and Human resource?
A: Purchasing is controlled by the Executive Chef (also Food and Beverage Director) and CFO. Each individual property chef does his or her own purchasing based on prescribed par-stock and his or her own receiving. The Executive Chef has support for HR activities by dedicated HR staff.

Q: Approximately how many different products you need to have in inventory to produce offered menu items?
A: Based on our inventory list, between 700 and 825, depending on season.

Q: When you design write or rewrite menus, do you put emphasis on cross utilisation?
A: Cross utilisation of product is not only a great concern for us in menu planning, but also for inventory management.

Q: How do you accomplish purchasing of various products?
A: We use a one-stop multiple product supplier as well as specialized suppliers and local suppliers for seasonal products

Q: With your product needs, can you incorporate the 100-mile rule of purchasing and are you concerned about the carbon footprint?
A: Our international clientele demands consistency in availability of certain products all the time, which makes the 100-mile rule and concern about carbon footprint a great challenge for us.

We do purchase available local/regional products whenever supply can be guaranteed.

Q: How do you deal with dead stock?
A: Stock from discontinued menu items will be utilised in buffets, chef's specials, and promotions.

Q: How do you manage purchasing considerations and control?
A: By reviewing daily, monthly, and to-date menu item usage reports sorted by category. These reports are created by our Remanco and Micros systems.

Inventory is taken monthly by two staff members, one receiver from the accounting department and one kitchen staff.

Q: What are your thoughts during the process of creating new (other than seasonal) menu items and in what way do you consider your customers while creating a menu item description?
A: I mandate that all food presentation must be of highest quality, have an appropriate colour combination, utilise a mix of cooking methods, be nutritious and visually appealing, and be aromatic with balanced seasoning. The creation of new (not seasonal) menu items is mainly driven by consumer demands for trends and my own desire to offer balanced and healthy choices. I personally communicate with customers to ensure if we serve their needs and address their expectations.

Q: How do you maintain a consistent plate presentation?
A: To ensure uniformity and portion control, plate presentations have been photographed and are posted at the pass (order and pick-up counter), in direct view of both the kitchen and the service staff to avoid accidental misinterpretation or misunderstandings.

Q: Do you adhere to a standard process (self-imposed or other) for creating a printable menu item description?
A: I impose guidelines on how to create explanatory descriptions in English, or words from a foreign language that are accepted in the English language. The usage of foreign words is limited to naming of dishes and must be explained in English. I want to ensure that my customers do not need to ask unnecessary questions, which may make them feel uncomfortable.

Q: Which method to calculate a menu selling price is your preferred method?
A: CPP (Cost per portion) divided by desired cost percentage.

Q: If staff would ask you what in your opinion is a good food cost percentage for your type of establishment(s), what would you tell them?
A: For our type(s) of establishments, the appropriate range of food cost would be: fine dining up to 38%, casual dining up to 31%, banquets up to 26%, average max 31.5%. If the average exceeds 32% based on standard sales mix, the reason will be investigated.

Q: Do you have a need and demand to follow trends?
A: We voluntarily follow food trends for cooking methods and presentations, especially trends toward healthy cooking, i.e., Acid and Alkaline balance, as well as modified fusion cooking.

Q: What influences you when making a selection of tableware to complement the food presentation as well as the atmosphere of the establishment?
A: Trends regarding tableware do not influence our standards unless specifically requested by the customer. In general we are looking for multipurpose, unadorned, and durable tableware.

Q: How frequently do you monitor the performance of offered menu items, and do you use a specific software for it?
A: Weekly and monthly, as well as seasonal menu mix evaluation. We analyse our Remanco and Micros reports for menu/sales mix, profitability, and popularity.

Q: What is your perception of and what do you expect from a "perfect menu"?
A: My perception and my expectation are quite similar: Menu items performing equally well because of their popularity, making the anticipated profit while being able to reduce quantity of items in inventory due to cross utilisation. I credit most of this to the feedback I solicit from our customers.

Q: Tony, for my final question; Do you have any other thoughts on menu planning for today's customer you would like to share with readers?
A: It is my firm belief that talking to our repeat customers as well transient travelers and amalgamating their expectations, and consequently trying our best to satisfied their needs and expectations, has contributed to the popularity of the brands we represent and our hotels in specific.

Acid Alkaline Menu — A story from its origins

Food consumption in the most advanced countries of the world has changed from nutritious raw food to highly processed foods that are very low in nutritional value. Our hunter-gatherer ancestors consumed a diet very different from what we would consider a typical diet today. Their diet was based on minimally processed plant and animal foods, however with the advent of agriculture the standard western diet has changed greatly. Enter the Alkaline Acid Diet- designed to emphasize fresh fruit, vegetables, roots and tubers, nuts and legumes. The new chemicals that have been added to our foods have put a greater stress on our systems ability to control the chemistry of our body's fluids. Therefore functionality of our inner biological terrain is at risk and as a result, we begin to see huge increases in the incidences of life threatening and chronic diseases. It is because of this that it is becoming more and more important to find an ideal balance of alkaline and acid forming foods.

The more alkaline-forming foods you add to your diet, the better results you will see. Should you not be able to completely avoid acidic foods, you should at least try to consume a very small amount and substitute acidic foods with more green food and vegetables.

The Crowne Plaza Toronto Airport, in support of a more healthy alkaline diet, has created a menu designed to identify the relative potential of high alkalinity (ph-level) existent in one ounce of food. The higher Ph-level a food has the higher potential of alkalinity the food may have and the healthier it is for you.

Remember that every little step towards a more alkaline diet is an improvement to a healthier way of life.

Market Fresh Vegetables

Cabbage (3.3), endive (14.5), romaine lettuce (2.2), celery (13.3), carrots (9.5), red radish(16.7), tomato (13.6), red onion (3.0), cucumber (31.5), avocado (15.6) and chives (8.3) tossed in extra virgin olive oil (1.0), fresh lemon juice (9.9) and garnished with pumpkin seeds (5.6), ground flax seeds (1.3) and almonds (3.6)

Beet & French Bean Salad

Gold beets (11.3), red beets (11.3), stripe beets (11.3), red onion (3.0), celery (13.3), garlic (13.2), chives (8.3), fennel seeds (1.3) and French beans (11.2) topped with watercress (7.7) and spinach (13.1). Tossed in extra virgin olive oil (1.0), fresh lemon juice (9.9) and garnished with ground flax seeds (1.3) and sunflower seeds (5.4)

Braised Cabbage roll with Tofu

Cabbage (3.3), tofu (3.2), red onion (3.0), garlic (13.2), chives (8.3), tomato (13.6), green peas (5.1), cumin seeds (1.1) with extra virgin olive oil (1.0) and almonds (3.6) braised in reduced tomato water and sprinkled with ground flax seeds (1.3) and toasted sesame seeds (0.5)

Navy Bean salad

Navy beans (12.1), red onion (3.0), garlic (13..2), celery (13.3), carrots (9.5), Brazil nuts (0.5), pumpkin seeds (5.6), sunflower seeds (5.4), figs (30.0) and baby spinach (13.1) tossed in extra virgin olive oil (1.0) and fresh lemon juice (9.9)

Baked Tofu mille feuille

Tofu (3.2), spinach (13.1), garlic (13.2), red onion (3.0), celery (13.3), fennel seeds (1.3), almonds (3.6), chives (8.3) and green peas (5.1) tossed in extra virgin olive oil (1.0) and accompanied with grilled asparagus (1.3), zucchini (5.7) and carrots (9.5). Served with tomato sauce (13.6)

DAVID GARCELON, EXECUTIVE CHEF

Melanie Coates.

David Garcelon, formerly Executive Chef at The Fairmont Royal York, was at the helm of Canada's largest hotel kitchen. He brought over 20 years of culinary experience to his brigade of over 110. From the kitchen he ensured that Fairmont's award-winning environmental program encourages guests to think green when traveling and dining by offering healthful and delicious menu choices that highlight organic products, VQA wines, and local purveyors. The hotel's on-site rooftop herb garden and apiary were natural extensions of his interest in sustainable food sourcing and purchasing. What Chef Garcelon's menus did do for the earth is just as important as what he expected his kitchens to deliver to the palate.

"As a Canadian Chef, I am thrilled to have returned to Canada and I am honoured to be given the opportunity to continue the long tradition of excellence in the kitchens of The Fairmont Royal York," says Garcelon. For Garcelon, the love of food began when he was 14 years old and took his first kitchen position. He grew up in St. Stephen, New Brunswick, and trained at the Culinary Institute of Canada in Charlottetown, PEI. Cooking his way up the culinary ladder, he started at the legendary hotel kitchen at the Windsor Arms Hotel in Toronto and then moved to the west coast and worked at the Westin Bayshore in Vancouver.

In 1993, Garcelon joined Canadian Pacific Hotels (now Fairmont Hotels & Resorts) and introduced the concept of regional cuisine to the Lodge at Kananaskis. In 1998 he became the Executive Chef at The Fairmont Jasper Park Lodge. The grand Canadian Rocky mountain resort is synonymous with superb cuisine and known among gourmands for its award-winning restaurants and menus inspired by local ingredients, seasons, and culinary heritage.

Chef Garcelon currently holds the position of Director of Culinary for the Waldorf Astoria Hotel, New York City, NY, USA.

"Our menu options reflect the best Canadian ingredients, with a commitment to seasonal, local, and sustainable products. In summer, meals are flavoured with herbs from our rooftop garden, where we are proud to cultivate our own unique varieties. This emphasis on freshness shows in every dish we create, from the healthy to the decadent, with the ultimate goal of creating inspiring options.

We aim to make your culinary event truly outstanding at The Fairmont Royal York."

Summary facts

The hotel features seven food outlets: The prestigious EPIC restaurant (160 B/100 L/80 D), the renowned Imperial Room (500 B/L/D), the Piper's Gastro Pub (80 D), the York's Deli and Bakery (250 B & L), as well as the York's Kitchen (250 B), the York Station (50 L) and the Library Bar (70 L & 60 D), In-Room Dining for 1365 rooms, and, it is the host for the famous Benihana Japanese restaurant (180 D).
Abbreviations used: Breakfast (B), Lunch (L), Dinner (D).
The combined seating capacity is 775 plus the Imperial Room (Banquets for 500) and 36 meeting/banquet facilities for a total of up to 4000.
Most menus for the various outlets will undergo changes about four times a year.

Interview

Q: On average, how many meals are produced daily?
A: Without banquets we serve daily approximately 1000 meals in the various outlets without the Benihana Restaurant, which operates on its own.

Q: How many Chefs, Sous Chefs, Station Chefs, and Cooks are in your brigade?
A: In order to deal with the daily production and banquets these positions report to me: 1 Kitchen Coordinator, 1 Executive Sous Chef, 1 Senior Sous Chef for the main kitchen, 1 Garde-Manger, 1 Avenues Sous Chef, 1 Senior Sous Chef banquets, 1 Epic Restaurant Chef, 1 Executive Pastry Chef, 1 Outlet Sous Chef, 1 Benihana Senior Teppan and Teppan Chefs and First Cook, 1 In-Room Dining, 2 Butchers, 1 Soup, 1 Sauce and Entremetier, 8 First Cooks, 8 Second Cooks, Apprentices and support staff, a total of 116 for three shifts.

Supporting departments are Human Resources, Maintenance, Catering, Graphic designer, and Director for banquets.

Q: Approximately how many different products you need to have in inventory to produce offered menu items?
A: For our daily needs we have approximately 500 different products in stock plus approximately 500 products for banquets as required.

Q: When you design, write, or rewrite menus, do you put emphasis on cross utilisation?
A: Absolutely; however, sometimes, based on customer demand, we will have to obtain single-use items.

Q: How do you accomplish purchasing of various products and are you able to incorporate the 100-mile rule of purchasing and are you concerned about carbon footprint?
A: We utilize a one-stop vendor, as well as about 100 independent vendors, based on our vision to use the freshest, seasonal, sustainable, and environmental friendly products.

Q: How do you deal with dead stock?
A: Fact is, because of our limited inventory and constraint purchasing habits and of course due to our high volume, dead stock has never been an issue. We are very product conscious and utilize as much as we can by doing our own stock and sauces, from the basics.

Q: How do you manage purchasing and receiving control?
A: We use now the FoodTrack software to control standard recipes, inventory, and purchasing. Purchasing is based on par stock and on banquet requirements. We have highly trained purchasers and receivers who check all shipments comparing to purchase orders. Due to our high volume and almost daily purchasing, we hardly need any freezers, which I consider to be graveyards for food.

Q: What are your thoughts during the process of creating new (other than seasonal) menu items and in what way do you consider your customers while creating a menu item description?
A: Demographics have taught us that our customers are in the 50- to 55-year-old corporate executive group, which are looking for high-quality mainstream staples, whereas the on the rise 40-plus executives and the increasing number of traveling female executives are looking for somewhat more fashionable, trendy, and healthy menu offerings.

Both groups demand a clear explanation of the offerings, identifying the key ingredients. The item description and the font style/type will complement the surroundings, from elegant to casual. Clear communication makes everyone's job easier, yet leaves room for the chefs to be creative with the plate presentation.

Q: How do you plan for and maintain consistent plate presentation?
A: The first step is to follow the standard recipe to ensure quality standards, which include taste and appropriate quantities. As I said before, I don't want to stifle the creativity of my chefs and I accept variations in the presentation, provided they have been communicated and everyone concerned is aware of them. Uniformity is important.

Q: Do you adhere to a standard process (self-imposed or other) in creating a printable menu item description?
A: Once again, the location the product is served in will determine the menu item description. By location I consider the whole makeup of the room, utensils and presentation plates and platter, table setup and the created atmosphere.

The actual layout of the menus is handled in-house with our own graphics department.

Q: Which method to calculate a menu selling price is your preferred method?
A: We use a variety of methods depending on the ingredient cost of the product to be sold. Prime cost is not normally used due to the fact that we are unionised and labour cost is basically a fixed cost. We are sensitive to our competition, yet we do offer the best to our customers and quality comes with a price tag. Interestingly enough, we have been, and I believe we still are, in Toronto the price-setters for banquets, meaning that other hotels will check our prices and try to stay in line with us.

Q: If your staff would ask you what in your opinion is a good food cost percentage for your type of establishment(s), what would you tell them?
A: Personally I do not like to quote an average or set percentage, since so much depends on the meal period, Breakfast, Lunch, Dinner, Afternoon Tea, and Banquets and on the product used. As you know, there is a considerable cost difference between the cost of a lobster, a steak, and a chicken, whereas the selling price may not reflect that difference. A lot depends on the sales mix.

Q: Do you have a need and demand to follow trends?
A: For some of our outlets the demand to follow trends is always there. Sophisticated customers look to New York and California for the latest culinary stimulation and excitement and have certain expectations when they come and dine with us. We keep informed by reading various magazines and Web-based news and of course with our connections to other industry professionals around the globe.

Q: What influences you when making a selection of tableware to complement the food presentation as well as the atmosphere of the establishment?
A: Being the establishment we are, we have a multitude of styles available to create or blend with different styles and atmospheres. However, on customer request we will rent anything the customer would like to have, budget depending.

Q: How frequently do you monitor the performance of offered menu items and do you use a specific method/software for it?
A: FoodTrack is the software we use for back of the house management, including Standard Recipes, Inventor, Purchasing, and Menu analysis. FoodTrack is linked with our Micros 9700 POS and enables us to get up-to-the-minute sales volume and menu mix reports.

Q: What is your perception of and what do you expect from a "perfect penu"?
A: I have a three-part answer for that: happy customers, happy owners, and happy cooks.

Q: Chef Garcelon, for my final question, if you were ever in the position to create a menu, without restrictions, what you would consider your personal favourite menu?
A: Yes, indeed I was, and I am happy to share this menu with you and your readers. The occasion was the hosting of the "Chapter of Confrérie de la Chaine des Rôtisseurs" on November 27, 2010. Throughout the menu we dedicated a course to the following Fairmont properties: The Fairmont Algonquin, The Fairmont Le Château Frontenac in Quebec, The Fairmont Château Laurier in Ottawa, The Fairmont Banff Springs, The Fairmont Empress in Victoria B.C., and last but not least the Fairmont Royal York in Toronto.

Note to readers; to view this menu please go to www.menuforprofit.com

Achievements

Chef Garcelon has enjoyed numerous awards and accolades from his peers in the culinary world, including:

- *Certified Chef de Cuisine Canada*
- *Slow Food member*
- *Certified Executive Chef USA*
- *2005 Chef of the Year Award, Bermuda Visitor Industry Partnership*
- *Bronze Medallion of Excellence, Bermuda Baillage Chaine des Rotisseurs*
- *Dish of the Year, Chaine des Rotisseurs, Alberta Nord*
- *United States Meat Export Federation Menu Competition Winner*
- *Bronze Medal National Team Hot Competition, Quebec City*
- *Canadian Champion's and Gold Medal Winner, Canadian Provincial Team Hot Competition*
- *Achieved 1st AAA Five-Diamond Award for The Newport Room Restaurant, Fairmont Southampton*
- *Achieved 1st AAA Four-Diamond Award for L'Escapade Restaurant, The Lodge at Kananaskis*

For the most up-to-date Fairmont Royal York Hotels menus please visit:
www.fairmont.com/EN_FA/Property/RYH/GuestServices/Restaurants/RestaurantsIndex

Tony Glitz

Photo courtesy of Tony Glitz.

As a member of Maple Leaf Sports and Entertainment renowned culinary team, Tony Glitz oversees Real Sports Bar and Grill as the Executive Chef. As a vital contributor to the opening team, Real Sports vowed to open its doors on June 15, 2010, and turn on its 199 HD screens, 39 ft big screen, 112 taps, and 50 ft long kitchen line for every fan who believes that style starts with a well-stitched jersey, that the number on your back isn't just a number, it's a legacy, and that he or she can watch the game on a two-story high, big-screen TV is a sports fan's given right.

Prior to joining Real Sports Bar and Grill, Glitz sharpened his culinary skills as the Executive Chef at Hawk's Cay Resort in the Florida Keys and eleven years with Four Seasons Hotels and Resorts encompassing Miami, Palm Beach, and Toronto. Being a direct descendant of cheese maker from Germany, Tony's father and grandfather were the pioneers in creating marble cheese, the original recipe being a combination of cheddar cheese curds and brick cheese in his hometown of Milverton, Ontario.

Additional culinary training came from a six-month internship in Kawaba, Japan, while graduating with honors from Humber College, where he received a degree in Culinary Management and Hotel and Restaurant Management.

Due to its enormous success and being voted the #1 Sports Bar in North America by ESPN, Real Sports Bar and Grill continues to expand with the Real Sports BBQ Pit at BMO field and a second restaurant in the development stages. For information on upcoming events, reservations, or to follow us on Twitter and Facebook, visit our website at Realsports.com

Establishment highlights

25,000 sq. ft, 899 seats, 2 floors, 199 HD TVs, the largest being 39 feet, voted the #1 Sports Bar in North America by ESPN

Open for lunch and dinner for à la carte, as well as breakfast, lunch, and dinner for catering.

The brigade, key positions, and hierarchy:

One Executive Chef, one Senior Sous Chef, 2 Sous Chefs, 4 Supervisors, 3 Lead Cooks, 26 Kitchen Workers, 16 Apprentices, and 15 Utility Attendants.

Number of shifts and kitchen staff for each shift:

Mise en place production over two shifts, 5 people each daily; Lunch; 8 people, 3 utility attendants; Dinner, 15 people, 6 utility attendants; Catering variable (staffed as needed)

Supporting departments:

Support cast from Air Canada Centre (ACC), Human Resources, Payroll, IT, Purchasing, Accounting, and PR

Interview

Q: How many different products you need to have in inventory to produce standard menu items?
A: We are getting daily delivery for any product, so we need only need to have just over 300 in inventory.

Q: Do you put emphasis on cross utilisation?
A: Always, it is vital for storage and for freshness of products.

Q: How do you deal with dead stock?
A: Tight ordering standards and knowing our par levels for the business at hand helps to shrink dead stock.

We make a daily staff meal, which works well, and we also contribute to Second Harvest for items we will not be able to use in time.

Q: What are your thoughts during the process of creating new (other than seasonal) menu items? i.e. what and why, including preparation challenges (staff, equipment), product and purchasing considerations, plate presentation, and service challenges.
A: First, brainstorming and testing if it can be managed within our current team. Second, it has to fit our clientele. Third, can I get the products I need to make it consistently great?

Then we write a starting recipe to test and tweak. We use multiple taste testing and getting the team's feedback and input, then check if it can be made in an effective manner that fits our fans and is cost effective.

Also important is the timing of the food to be made, and can it be made at a pace to serve the guests in a timely manner.

Q: In what way do you consider your customers while creating a menu item description?
A: It's all about the fans and the service staff. If the staff does not like it, they will not recommend it. If the fans do not like it, they will never order it again.

Q: Are you affected by, and if so, how do you deal with the impact of demographic changes?
A: Our restaurant has the ability to cater to all types of sports fans. We have hockey days, basketball days, baseball days, European soccer days, and football days, and many times multiples happen on the same days. Our philosophy is, we will always show the live events first, and then we listen to our fans what is the most popular. Having 199 TVs, it is easy to locate a TV for any fan who wants something different. Our mix of menu items is suitable to, or respectively, not affected by changing demographics.

Q: What process (self-imposed or other) you adhere to while creating a printable menu item description?
A: Our menu is very unique and tells a great story. Having 85 menu items, there is lots to choose from. There are many inspirational quotes that give you a feeling of being a part of something big. When it comes to the descriptions, layout, and grammar, I tend to be the last person to say yes to it. I am kind of controlling that way as I do not believe in spelling mistakes, EVER!

Q: Which one is your preferred method to calculate a menu selling price?
A: My costing method is quite variable per item. It is important to do a thorough market analysis of your competitors in the area and understand you cannot be above or below by a huge margin. Once a percentage has been set for a menu, I run it through several previous months

of product mix based on previous sales to give an honest calculation of what the monthly food cost will look like in the upcoming months so I can speak intelligently and with authority to why the food cost is following certain trends.

Q: If your staff would ask you, what in your opinions is a good food cost percentage for your type of establishment, what would you tell them?
A: 30 to 35%. Often the food cost can swing a little based on our product mix. This can happen by selling more of certain dishes that do not have a high margin. Catering and events can also affect our food cost due to a lower food cost % on large functions. So at the end of the month, it can change based on what was sold.

Q: Do you like to follow, or have a need and demands to follow, trends?
A: Yes, it important to stay current on what is happening and continue to let the menu evolve over time to keep it fresh and inviting. Variety is the spice of life.

Q: What influences you when making a selection of tableware/flatware to complement the food presentation as well as the atmosphere of the establishment?
A: Durability, recognizability, and fun. Many times a menu item will evoke different emotions just by the plate that it is on. Sometimes it must be classic and sometimes it must be daring, but do not be afraid to try something different.

Q: Your thoughts about seasonal menu items, impact on slow food, 100-mile menu, and carbon footprint?
A: Seasonal menus are great for specials and for smaller establishments. However, with 85 menu items, it can be hard to keep the proper products available for consistency.

Q: How frequent do you monitor the performance of offered menu items and do you use a specific software or system to accomplish this task?
A: We go through formal sous chef tastings of a few items before lunch and dinner every day. This is for us to test, evaluate, and give feedback on the dish regarding how it was made, presentation, and if anything was lacking. This is logged into our tasting log for future reference. It is crucial that we are consistent in our food, no matter who cooks it. The best way to do so is to taste it.

We also rely on our daily P- Mix, which gives a strong indication of our performance. This same data is used at the end of the month to calculate theoretical food cost, which is a valuable tool on where you should be tracking.

Q: What is your perception of and what do you expect from a "perfect menu"?
A: Spelling, a story, and variety. I do not go out of my way to see spelling mistakes, but I am very conscious of them. A menu needs to be fun and evoke an emotional connection with the guest. You want them to be able to think about how it tastes before they get it, and then you have to deliver the "WOW!" By knowing your fans, you should be able to target their favourites, not yours. Then you have to ensure the costs are in line so you can have a healthy and sustainable restaurant.

Q: Tony, for my final question, what advice on menu planning for today's customer would you like to give to readers?
A: When planning a menu, don't take it personally, but make it personable. It should be easy to read and navigate, while having a little fun and enticing customers to buy because they gotta try it.

The current R/S Real Sports Bar and Grill menu is at:
www.realsports.ca/bar/menu
www.e11even.ca/menus

MARK JACHECKI CCC,EXECUTIVE CHEF

Photo courtesy of Mark Jachecki

MISSION STATEMENT

Empowerment is the key for a successful operation. With a progressive management style and proactive leadership, a positive morale is achieved. Using organization and positive communication, the kitchen team knows and understands the internal and external guest. This creates the forum for modern cuisine where the food will lead the way.

As past leader of the eight Canyon Creek Chophouse® restaurants in the Greater Toronto Area, Executive Chef Mark Jachecki relies on his enviable combination of European roots, classic training, and award-winning culinary experience to bring innovative menu ideas to the table that keep guests coming back for more.

With more than twenty years of experience at hotels both small and large, in restaurants both contemporary and classic, with groups from two to 5,000, this 40-plus-year-old accomplished chef has been able to collect his considerable talents to pilot the culinary operations of the growing chain of Canyon Creek restaurants, managing approximately 100 kitchen staff that serve thousands of meals each day.

Since joining Canyon Creek in late 2007, Jachecki has achieved several milestones. Among them, he opened the Canyon Creek Toronto Airport location and has installed a number of highly successful seasonally inspired menus across all Canyon Creek locations, including a comprehensive fall 2009 program that affiliated Canyon Creek with more than fifteen local farmers and growers. According to Jachecki, the experience of embracing the local food movement was very rewarding—and one he plans to duplicate and expand in the near future.

"As a chef I'm proud to say Canyon Creek has had a positive impact on sustaining Ontario's growing industry. We really introduced our guests to the eat-local approach, helping them to understand that it isn't just a lofty idea, but it can be done affordably and with great-tasting results. Supporting local farms is very rewarding and I think it's clear using farm fresh food is the right thing to do. I'm looking forward to embracing more of the wonderful foods that grow in our own backyard, because that's the key to really staying fresh—by working locally to achieve it."

Since childhood, Jachecki has been exposed to the culinary life. As a boy, he was introduced to the wonders of the kitchen through the beloved German restaurant, Zum Rhein, located in Toronto on Lakeshore Boulevard West, which was owned by his father in the late 1970s to early

1980s. Jachecki's grandfather was also a Toronto chef at the prestigious Granite Club originally located on St. Clair Avenue West.

Those family influences led Jachecki to begin his cooking career in the classic European tradition of a rigorous apprenticeship at Toronto's Regal Constellation Hotel (1987–1990). There, his affinity with the hotel's Swiss chef and the classic French Escoffier methods he was being taught inspired Jachecki's own Swiss experience at Gasthof Sternen hotel in Wettingen in 1991.

Upon his return to Canada later that year, Jachecki took the lead as chef of dining rooms of The Estates of Sunnybrook (Vaughan Estate) for six years, before joining the award-winning restaurant 360 at the CN Tower for two years. In 1988, he was named top toque at one of Toronto's premier hotels, The Westin Harbour Castle, and was most recently the chef of a successful catering company for seven years before joining Canyon Creek.

A Certified Chef de Cuisine (CCC – American Culinary Federation), Jachecki resides in Markham, Ontario, and is a Vice President of Les Toques Blanches, and member of The American Culinary Federation, The Escoffier Society, and Les Chaines de Rotisseurs.

ABOUT CANYON CREEK CHOPHOUSE

Canyon Creek Chophouse www.canyoncreekchophouse.com is a casual yet premium dining experience ideal for lunch, dinner or late night dining. Winning décor and excellent service are met with outstanding, simple cuisine, squarely focused on classic items with a twist including premium cuts like rack of lamb, sirloin steak and cedar plank salmon. Canyon Creek Chophouse first opened in 1997 and currently has eight locations across Southern Ontario including Canyon Creek Airport, Burlington, Etobicoke, Front Street, Mississauga, Niagara Falls, Scarborough and Vaughan Mills.

ABOUT SIR CORP. – SERVICE INSPIRED RESTAURANTS

SIR Corp. ("SIR") is a privately held Canadian corporation that owns and operates a portfolio of 45 casual and fine dining restaurants in Canada. The business is focused on creating, developing, and operating best-in-class restaurants. Best-in-class means SIR strives for the best people, the best food, and the best atmosphere at each of its restaurants. These values are shared company-wide and the resulting high level of quality and attention to detail can be found in each restaurant. SIR's passion is reflected in its name, which stands for Service Inspired Restaurants.

SIR is about bringing people together, building lasting relationships, and setting the standard for best in class. SIR has grown from five restaurants and $17 million in revenue in 1993 to 45 restaurants and over $197 million in revenue in its fiscal year ending August 30, 2009.

Currently, SIR has approximately 3,800 employees across Canada. SIR's diverse portfolio of restaurants is designed to appeal to a broad set of consumer tastes. Concept restaurants have multiple locations, reflecting their broader demographic appeal.

SIR concept brands include Jack Astor's® Bar and Grill, with 29 locations in Canada; Alice Fazooli's!®, with five locations; and Canyon Creek Chop House®, with eight locations. SIR's Signature Restaurants are one-of-a-kind brands located in downtown Toronto that range in offerings from fine dining with award-winning menus to a very active sports bar. Signature Restaurants comprise the upscale reds®, Far Niente®, Four™, Petit Four™ and the casual Loose Moose Tap & Grill®. All trademarks related to the concept and signature brands noted above are used by SIR under a license agreement with SIR Royalty Limited Partnership. For more information on SIR Corp. or the SIR Royalty Income Fund, please visit www.sircorp.com.

Interview

Q: Although it is already stated in the press release, how many outlets are under your supervision? What are the number of seats for each outlet and meal periods for the various outlets (i.e., breakfast, lunch, afternoon tea, dinner) and number of meals produced (daily average)?
A: At Canyon Creek we currently have 8 restaurants from Niagara to Scarborough. Each restaurant serves approximately 2000 guests per week. They vary in size from about 90 seats to 140 seats. We operate from 11:30 to some locations 1:00 AM, 7 days a week for lunch and dinner service.

Q: What is the structure of the brigade, key positions and hierarchy, number of shifts and kitchen staff for each shift and what type of supporting departments—i.e., Purchasing, Stewarding, Food & Beverage Control, and Human Resources—are available to you?
A: I run the food program as the Concept or Corporate Chef. The brigade is chiefly run on a day-to-day operation by a Chef of each restaurant, some having a Sous Chef and then we have line cooks. Since we are a steak house, the majority of the flair is required off the grill. The positions we have are Grill (chef d'partie), Sautee (poissonnier, entremétier), Pantry (Larder – hot and cold appetizers and dessert). We have a preparation kitchen where we make 90% of the products from scratch, all of our own desserts and cut our own lettuce, so Garde-manger is covered here. We have our stewards act as dishwashing, receivers, extra prep cooks (training), and what we call "curb to curb" duties, which take care of the surrounding area of the restaurant (parking lot, receiving doors, sanitation). The front of house management team is run by the restaurant General Manager, with a Beverage Manager, and Floor Managers. For the most part, all controls and systems are handled by the General Manager and Chef as well as in restaurant Human Resource duties.

Q: How do you accomplish purchasing of the various products? Does your product need allow for the 100-mile rule of purchasing and are you concerned about the carbon footprint?
A: We try to do one-stop shopping. We try to use one company for meats/seafood, one for dry goods and freezer, one company for produce. It works quite well as we like to keep an eye on the carbon footprint and also keep delivery charges at a minimum. This being said, our supplier partners work very hard in carrying items for us (that they do not commonly stock) because they are already delivering to our back door. There are occasions where they cannot and then we need a special supplier—this is rare, but ever changing. At Canyon Creek one of the philosophies I have is that I really want Farm Centric menu items, so that we can tell where they are from. In this spirit I first look at local, then provincial, and then Canadian product well before the world market, or the cheapest product out there. This is very important.

Q: What are your thoughts during the process of creating new (other than seasonal) menu items?
A: This is a great question as we (May 2011) have just gone through creating a new menu—we are a steak house and that is our "meat and potatoes," but I look at the whole business, from what is important to our people, to having fun at cooking and offering new foods. Looking at the very competitive casual dining market and wanting to offer different flavours for our bar guests and diners, yet staying true to company values and promise and brand identity is a challenge.

I would do this with our team of chefs while utilizing our current kitchen footprint and equipment to design the menus. It is our people/cooks who will need to make the food and execution of any new menu the success. There are always challenges with new directions and preparation, space, and execution, but it's a restaurant. It is a living and breathing thing.

Q: How do you and in what way do you consider your customers while creating menu item descriptions and how do you deal with the impact of demographic changes?
A: Before I create menus I walk the restaurants, see what guests like, pull the numbers, and see what sells (and make sure they are priced effectively). I speak with guests about what we are planning. I just started with social media and Twitter some ideas and people submit back their opinions on things. It is very interesting and often works for me.

Demographic changes are an important part. Basically we are working on a core menu and then adding some different touches/offerings at different restaurants to accommodate. There are not vastly different menus, just a few items, but I think this matters.

Q: Do you adhere to a standard process (self-imposed or other) while creating a printable menu item description?
A: Yes we do, we believe it needs to be consistent throughout Canyon Creek in how we present it to the guest, but we are always testing new, possibly better, ways to do this.

Q: Which method to calculate a menu selling price is your favourite?
A: Actual cost pricing and gross profit method are the most common. We are not really in the market for prestige pricing or cost plus. We use a computer program, but I still double check it all with pencil and paper—old school.

Q: If kitchen staff would ask you what is a good food cost for your type of establishment, what would you tell them?
A: A good food cost is 32% because we are a steakhouse and protein costs are the centre plate champion. If we buy well and market conditions are on our side, 31% would be great. More often than not we are closer to 33%, which is textbook.

Q: Approximately how many different products you need to have in inventory to produce offered standard menu items? Do you put emphasis on cross utilisation, and how do you deal with dead stock?
A: We have about 500 items. When I design items for the menu, I of course try to utilize already existing products; however, I find that if you do not offer new menu items on a rotating basis, you run the risk of designing your operation to be like the "JENGA" game. So when you want to list new foods something will suffer as everything is almost overutilized. There is a fine line of cross utilization and carving everything in stone as it will at some point be too difficult to change and offer your guests new things.

Dead stock, for the most part, we utilize it with features or create something we can offer our guests to augment their experience in our restaurants.

Q: Your thoughts about seasonal menu items, impact on slow food, 100-mile menu and carbon footprint?
A: We do a local harvest promotion every fall and every year see more and more of these items make our core menu. We buy as local as possible using tomatoes from Leamington 10 months of the year, buying carrots from Holland Marsh from my budding Jason at Carron Farms, and I use the resources of John Bishop at Fresh Start foods to help me find local brokers to buy their product and have it delivered to all eight Canyon Creeks. We have used companies like 100-mile market and use many suppliers that are recognized by Local Foods Plus. So we do not preach 100-mile or organic, what we focus on is Farm Centric items so we can tell everyone where we get our products from and first look at Ontario for product. If shrimp ever come to Ontario, I will try them!

Q: How do you and how frequently do you monitor the performance of offered menu items? Do you use a specific software or system to accomplish this task?
A: We have a food costing program linked to our point of sale system to get menu mixes and preference results and average food costing on a daily weekly and per period basis.

Q: Do you like to follow, or have a need and demand to follow, trends?
A: I am aware of and follow trends; however, we currently try what is tested and true but use the current trends for restaurant features.

Q: What influences you when making a selection of tableware to complement the food presentation as well as the atmosphere of the establishment?
A: I look at my selections in the restaurant in the proper lighting on the table. I personally like square plates, but at Canyon Creek they will not work on the table. I look at the table and how much space new china will take up in front of the guest. In analysing the flatware, the most comfortable in a ladies hand works the best.Except for the steak knife, it is big!

Q: What is your perception of and what do you expect from a "perfect menu"?
A: I personally like a well-balanced menu, very simple, like each menu item, something that is the hero item, something savoury and sweet, something that is soft, and something crunchy. Category management of a menu (as a generalization) for your concept of food is the most important thing to look at and when 30% of people eat fish, 30% people each chicken, 30% people eat steak, and the rest have your features, 50% have and appetizer, 50% have a dessert and coffee—you have the perfect penu.

I have yet to see a perfect menu, but this is what we as chefs strive for.

Q: Chef, for my final question, what other thoughts you may have on menu planning for today's customer that you would like to share with readers?
A: Being a Chef seems like a very easy thing to most people. Everybody has the ability to cook something. Therefore everybody is an expert in his or her own way. This is different from any other industry that I know. Not everyone has a green thumb, not everyone can do plumbing or trade stocks or heal people. I think that you could serve 100 the same dish in a night; 80 people would love it, 10 people would like it, and 10 people would not like it at all.

I think it best that as a customer you should find out the offerings of the restaurant as an all-round experience and then make your decision about where to go to be entertained. I have heard many chefs say, "wait a moment… good food takes time…," and this is true, but it is the guest's experience from entering the restaurant, to being greeted with a smile, to having a gentle picture painted of the items he or she has selected to eat and drink, to getting a close rendition of the picture and having it packaged with an ambiance you would expect. Menu planning is the infrastructure for this and a well-planned menu benefits the customer, the establishment, and all the people involved in bringing food from field to fork.

For the latest Canyon Creek Chophouse Menus please visit:
www.canyoncreekchophouse.com/locations_airport.php?type=menu

Brian Morin, Owner and Executive Chef of the beerbistro

Mike McColl @ www.photoswithsauce.ca

Photo credit: Mike McColl @ www.photoswithsauce.ca

From the beerbistro's website; message in a bottle...

Call this our Six Year Itch. Over the whole time that we've been open, never before have we sought out and acquired more new and tempting beers. And we're not just going after the young ones, either. This latest menu features our most expansive cellar list yet, including ridiculously rare and tasty vintages beers never before seen in Ontario.

This time, our focus has been on bringing in bottles from some of the most extraordinary breweries throughout the United States. Of particular note are all three beers from Avery Brewing's acclaimed Demons of Ale series. On a scale of one to ten, with one being jumping out of an airplane without a parachute and ten being trampled by a herd of angry mastodons, these beers rank about an eight.

For those who worship the hop, here's some communion for you: Sierra Nevada's Harvest Ale—brewed with fresh, resinous hops picked that very same day, and Port Brewing's Hop 15—a beer that throws in everything including the kitchen sink, provided said kitchen sink is made of hops and also filled with hops.

Included in this enormous release are also some bottles of refined and subtle character. In a brewing world fascinated by the depths of human sensory tolerance, we've got some standouts showing mastery in the art of restraint. Anderson Valley's Barney Flats Oatmeal Stout comes to mind, as does the golden and spicy Carnevale from Lost Abbey.

Enjoy reading through the beer list. Thanks for reading, and treat yourself to something new before we drink it all ourselves. Cheers.

As a restaurateur in the heart of Toronto my restaurant performs a dual role; during lunch time I am patronized by the Bay Street (Financial district) crowd, and in the evening I am a neighbourhood restaurant.

Recently, I revamped all my menus to achieve my goal, which is to offer an unpretentious, relaxed atmosphere in which clients feel comfortable sharing the menus items among them. I noticed that people are now choosing differently, from every area on the menu. Since that change, the average check has gone up 2 to 3 dollars. To be as "seasonal" as possible the menus are changed four times a year and beers are matched with the menus. Like for now with summer approaching we feature more crisp beer. My cooks and I have quite successfully started to make our own cheeses. Right now we make about four types and with every successful new type, we are encouraged to try another new one. It is fun to make cheeses. I have learned doing cheeses by reading about it, trying it, making mistakes until I finally succeeded, which encourages me to continue trying to make different cheeses.

Besides me being in the kitchen, I have working with me 1 Chef, 3 Sous Chefs, Cooks, and seven Apprentices.

Our beer offerings include about 140 bottles and twenty on tap. Most beers I buy age very well. Translated into dollars, we have about 100,000 in beer inventory. Demands for different, new, and what you may call it exotic beer keep increasing.

To keep my staff abreast of new additions and also as a refresher, they are encouraged to attend a monthly update. We offer a beer school for the staff every two weeks; staff is informed of new additions and is able to taste them. Following the tasting they must describe the beers. Our staff's knowledge enables them to make affirmative recommendations to a guest who says, "I like Alexander Keith. What do you suggest?" Staff will know what to answer. We learned that the clients appreciate being guided, and we love being able to help people with the selection of beer— how to pour different beers correctly into glasses. The type of glass used is important to the proper presentation of beer—some glasses are better suited for some beers than for others. Stephen Beaumont and I have made a great effort in explaining beer types, the selection of the right glass, and the proper pouring based on the type of beer, and of course, how to cook with beer in our book *The beerbistro Cookbook*, published by Key Porter Books, www.keyporter.com ISBN# 1-55470-140-6. Signed copies are available in the restaurant.

Although I keep my menu in a plastic cover and it appears to be casual, it is still elegant in its presentation and my writing style addresses my customers. They are very comfortable with it.

Because on weekends and in the evening I am a neighbourhood restaurant, I tried to come up with a brunch menu—my goal was to be in the top 10 restaurants for brunch in the city. Although I loved the idea, I had to cancel brunch because of the food cost.

We try to maintain a food cost between 28% and 30%, which is quite achievable since we make everything in house fresh from scratch. In my opinion menus have to be displayed as per the product market prices, meaning I do not gauge the client, I pay top dollar for the best raw product available. Meaning, if you have a really nice menu people may think it is too expensive to eat at your establishment.

Menus are printed on selected premium medium-heavy stock at Staples. Brian gives them a pdf proof for printing. It is cheaper to do it this way if you change your menus often. They are easy to maintain and change and they stand up better with the plastic cover—menus last two to three months then they are changed.

The answer to your question "What do you think of the evolving ipad menu?" I am not in favour of it, yet. A traditional menu you can over-see one to two pages easily; on a electronic tablet you would have to scroll up and down and flip pages to get the same information. If you do not know how to use these electronic gadgets, you may feel intimidated. I don't think they are user friendly enough for some clients.

I truly believe in Facebook and Twitter, i.e., I beer-marinate and smoke my own salmon. When the younger crowd client tastes it, they put their comments on Facebook and Twitter—there is no better publicity. It is personal, has a pyramid effect, and is truly powerful. Blogs are so important and I compare them to a food writer writing an article in the newspaper.

Interview

Q: You possess an extensive knowledge about beer. How did you acquire it?

A: I studied beer the same way you would study wine. The big difference is that wine is mainly up to the weather gods, whereas to make beer, you need to mix your desired ingredients in appropriate proportions and apply your technical skills and equipment to ferment and brew. With beer you can create your own recipe and have consistency. Brewmasters are like chefs.

Q: Do you and your staff adhere to a Standard Recipe format and does everybody follow recipes?
A: All our recipes have been tested and tweaked to perfection, and staff strictly follows recipes. Between pan, grill section, gardemanger, and tournant, we prepare on average of 400 to 500 covers, depending on day of the week and the time of the year. In the summer we open the patio with additional 70 seats. There is no room for personal interpretation of a recipe—consistency in ingredients, method of preparation, taste, presentation, quality, and quantity is a must.

Although not everyone drinks beer, beer consumption is directly influenced by the weather. As it gets warmer, consumption increases.

The staffing of the kitchen, which is not very large, yet fast paced, is designed for efficiency. The majority kitchen staff are line cooks, still attending school, working in one week four days on line, eliminating prep cooks. Sous Chefs do full time prep and three days on the line. It is the Sous Chef's responsibility to ensure that recipes are followed—consistency is the most important thing for me.

Q: How do you select new staff to complement the brigade?
A: To complement the brigade, new hires are not only hired for their skills and personality, they are selected for their attitude. It is most important to me. Skills I can teach.

I rotate kitchen staff ongoing—2 to 3 years max—and then it is time to leave the restaurant and see something else. I suggest they should leave—they have just graduated from the Beer Bistro. They have learned all there is to learn, now it is time to go and see something else. Although high quality, we make casual food. I encourage them to go and work in a banquet hall or hotel or large restaurant. This learning process has a big impact on their career. I strongly suggest that the apprentices do not take shortcuts.

Like this, the staff get to see how we do all the menu items. I love to be in control of all our food. To accomplish this, I am constantly learning new things. Recently I got more involved with bread making and with baking in general, and now we make all our own breads and cakes. Not only is this very satisfying, it also makes me more independent from suppliers. As you can see, I like to be in control of my own food—and I like to make it from scratch. This is beer cuisine: 90% of products we make contain beer, i.e. Blanche de Chambly beer for smoked salmon.

Q: How do you manage purchasing and Inventory control?
A: The Sous Chef does the purchasing; I personally sign all the cheques.Some of the purchasing is done by the manager of the restaurant.

Q: Approximately how many different products you need to have in inventory to produce offered menu items?
A: Approximately 1000 items, seasonally adjusted depending on the product. Because of the small spaces, we try to limit our products such as vinegars to maybe four kinds only.

Q: When you design, write, or rewrite a menu, do you put emphasis on cross utilisation?
A: I am very concerned with cross utilization. Limited production and storage space demands my attention to each product and its adaptability to be used in more than one menu offering.

Q: How do you manage the purchasing process of needed products?
A: I created an order guide line for every single item category, separated by suppliers—i.e., all the cheeses are from the Cheese Boutique except for the ones I make myself. I do not order from one-stop suppliers. The cost of product is obviously a concern, but I would rather trade cost for sourced quality products rather than for lowest price. I selfishly have control of every product we purchase.

When in season, I dehydrate pears, plums, and peaches, make preserves, and restore them in winter time. The flavours are often more intense and perfectly suited to complement cheese trays and other menu offerings. You just cannot buy a full-flavoured peach in the winter.

Q: Can you incorporate the 100-mile rule of purchasing and are you concerned about the carbon footprint?
A: I would love to say yes; however, reality is, I will when I can and will not when I cannot. 100-mile rules would be great if they would include California and Spain, for example. How could I offer Australian beer or Columbian coffee? I love to support sustainable farms, but it is difficult for me. I tried to use grass-fed beef, but the small abattoir we selected offered slaughter only every two weeks, and consistency could not be achieved. I strongly dislike any frozen products (except ice cream), so this concept did not work for me. Once I select a supplier I stick with it because I want to have assurance of consistency.

Q: What are your thoughts during the process of creating new (other than seasonal menu) menu items, and how do you consider your customers while creating a menu item description?
A: All our menus are seasonal. Menus are changed four times a year. I listen to the customer, and the new menu format with the "to share" section is mainly based on the feedback from our customers.

I am somewhat meticulous in the process. When I create a new menu, I know that I will have to have a chicken, salmon, steak dish, and additional items to give the flavour of the restaurant, casual dining segment: Caesar salad, house salad, chicken wings, buggers, blts—some items became staples on the menus. One example would be pulled pork; we were very cautious when we introduced the item, as it turned out, we now use four shoulders a week, we buy it bone in, and prepare one batch per week. I started to make my own ketchup. It is a lengthy but worthwhile process using fresh tomatoes, lime juice, and sugar.

Q: Are demographics a concern for your establishment?
A: Our location is quite unique—we cater to different clientele throughout the day. We try to attract young professionals and satisfy late night and weekend needs. Our target market is 25 to 40 years old— customers in this age range have a different attitude, more willing to explore the non-standard menu offerings.

Q: Do you adhere to a standard process, self-imposed or otherwise, in creating a printable menu item description?
A: Absolutely. I like to use fun names for the items. The title should reflect on the key ingredient(s). I prefer not to romance the items. If the customer is uncertain, the server can explain, encouraging customer and server interaction. For example, pork is supplied by the Mennonites. This fact is not mentioned on the menu, but the server will emphasise this fact while interacting with the customer.

Q: Which method to calculate a menu selling price is your preferred method?
A: I created a beer pricing spreadsheet that rates the product from 1 to 6. Because the cost to me is strictly regulated, I need to keep a 20% to 35% beverage cost, which helps the cost of the many imported beers.

Depending on the food items, most of the time contribution margin is favoured over cost percentage. For products that are benchmarked items for competitive products, I obviously need to be very sensitive to the menu pricing. Some items just must be in line with the market. Our main client base is from the nearby hotels, businesses, and condos.

My labour cost is about 33%. We can keep the labour cost around this percentage because we are doing the sales numbers. Today we have over 50 employees, 7 days a week. When I first opened the restaurant we employed 17 persons.

Q: If your staff would ask you what you consider to be a good food cost percentage, what would you tell them?
A: I budget for 31.5% average year-round with seasonal adjustments based on price of non-seasonal items. All chefs should know what costs are involved in running the whole restaurant, not only the kitchen.

Q: Do you have a need or demand to follow trends?
A: I would say so—we need to satisfy the public demands.

Q: What influences you when making a selecting table or silver ware to complement the food presentation as well as the atmosphere of the establishment?
A: I believe that chinaware and presentation are of equal value to the customer. Most of our dishes are white, to let the food to speak for itself. The shape and proportion of the product determines what we present it on. We use elegant, yet durable, stainless steel cutlery and large coffee cups.

Q: How often do you monitor the performance of menu items and do you use specific software for that function?
A: I use the report functions from our Squirrel system, which give me the sales and the menu mix information. Knowing my costs, I can complete any analysis.

Q: What is your definition and expectation of a "perfect menu"?
A: I am happy with our menu. I am proud of what I have created.It satisfies my customers. The perfect menu should be one you can take to the bank and also pleases the guests. It should limit offerings and feature quality products. All items in inventory should be turning over quickly so that products are always fresh and be small enough in number that your establishment is able to prepare all items comfortably.

Q: Chef, for my final question, what other thoughts on menu planning for today's customer do you have and would like to share with readers?
A: For a menu that satisfies and makes the customer happy, you must be very proud of the menu and the products you offer. You must have pride to do things from scratch use your skills, hands, and senses. I am here for hospitality. You may name me what I am—a servant who is not fulfilled unless his master, the customer, is happy. I don't mind being a well-paid and respected servant.

Q: Do you have any advice for a young cook?
A: Move around and learn before you become a Sous Chef.

Q: At what time in your life should you write a menu?
A: When you become a Sous Chef, or when your position requires you to be responsible. I encourage all my cooks to offer their opinion on specials and menu items. I consider their opinion, but I will have the final word what is written on the menu.

Brian, using his own advice to others, reformatted the bistro's menu with his Chef Michelle's input. Since this revision the average check has noticeable increased!

Brian Morin, thank you for your insights. I wish you and your business continued success.

For the beerbistro's most recent menu postings please visit:

www.beerbistro.com/index.php/menus

Timothy Palmer, Chef of the Restaurant in the Royal York Hotel Toronto

Melanie Coates.

Mr. Palmer started his apprenticeship at the Fairmont Jasper Park Lodge in the Rocky Mountains and attended SAIT College in Calgary as well as NAIT College in Edmonton. He entered several competitions and was awarded recognition from the Chaîne des Rôtisseurs and Alberta Beef. After working as Chef de Cuisine in Fairmont's Jasper Park Lodge's Four Diamond Edith Cavell Dining Room, he relocated to Queensland, Australia, to become the Banquet Chef at the Sheraton Mirage Resort in Port Douglas.

In 2007 he rejoined the Fairmont family in Bermudas Fairmont Southampton hotel to become the Chef de Cuisine in the Four Diamond Waterlot Inn Steak House. It was there were he created his signature dishes using classical and local cooking techniques. Mr. Palmer is committed to making environmentally friendly choices for all menu items and follows the 100-mile rule whenever possible. At the EPIC restaurant, local, sustainable, and seasonal ingredients are always the menu highlights.

In 2010 Mr. Palmer arrived at the Royal York Hotel from Bermuda to become the Executive Chef for the EPIC restaurant, which has as a reputation for innovation and quality. The menu features the best of Ontario growers and utilizes herbs and honey from its own herb garden located 14 stories above street level on the hotel's rooftop. The EPIC restaurant is a certified Ocean Wise restaurant.

Under the tutelage of the Royal York Hotel Executive Chef David Garcelon, Mr. Palmer and his team created the following menus.

Please download our breakfast, lunch, dinner, and dessert menus for more detail.

All menu items and prices are subject to change.

www.fairmont.com/royalyork/GuestServices/Restaurants/Epic.htm

Raimund A. Zyvatkauskas, CCC Executive Chef

Matt Pozdrowski.

A music student and second-generation chef, Chef Raimund Zyvatkauskas is deeply passionate about food and cooking. He believes a great meal requires both quality ingredients and superb craftsmanship. The wide range of menus at Kingbridge reflects a depth of experience and collaboration with his team.

Chef Raimund started his career as a teenager working in a boutique hotel, then later apprenticed in a five-star thousand-room hotel in Toronto. Chef Raimund later went on to become Executive Chef of the largest hotel in Canada. He has designed, built, and opened several new kitchens and successful new concept restaurants.

Previously voted the Chef of the year for the Greater Toronto area by his peers, Raimund recently chaired the Canadian Culinary Institute for the Escoffier Society. Raimund is a past-Chair of the Culinary Advisory board for George Brown College and has sat on the advisory board for hospitality programs at Centennial College.

Advancing the profession through training is one of Raimund's priorities. Over the years he has mentored many young cooks who have gone on to become successful chefs. He believes in life-long learning and is constantly advancing his own skills through courses and study.

Chef Raimund's approach to menu writing is to first seek to understand the audience, then gather information from those around you, and finally to work in collaboration with the entire team to write menus that are first honest "a menu description should give the guest an honest idea of what to expect." He also prefers to keep the use adjectives or flowery speech out of descriptions. When appropriate, such as on buffets or sometimes in footnotes, he likes to tell a story of where ingredients are from or the history of an item. In this way the menu tells a story and provides a learning opportunity. Raimund also regularly shares his culinary expertise and recipes with guests of the Kingbridge Conference Centre and Institute.

Interview

Q: Please tell me the types of establishment, number of outlets within the establishment, number of seats for each outlet, and meal periods for the various outlets (i.e., Breakfast, Lunch, Afternoon Tea, Dinner) as well as number of meals produced (daily average) broken down by outlets.

A: The Kingbridge Centre and Institute is a dedicated conference centre with a 200-seat dining room, 100-seat bar and lounge, and over 24,000 square feet of meeting space. The dining room typically serves 100-plus for breakfast, 200-plus for lunch and about 150-plus for dinner. Banquets fluctuate according to guest needs; we have done banquets as large as 750 for lunch and as small and intimate as less than 10. We are a three-meal period plus break stations operation that runs seven days a week.

Q: How many employees are in your kitchen brigade, what are their key positions and hierarchy, number of shifts, and kitchen staff for each shift and type of supporting departments, i.e. Purchasing, Stewarding, Food & Beverage Control, and Human Resources?

A: Our brigade consists of one Executive Chef, one Executive Sous Chef, three Chef de Parties, three First Cooks, two Second Cooks, and five third Cooks. This property has a fairly flat management structure with each department including Culinary looking after its own purchasing.

Stewarding and Receiving are part of the culinary team. We work closely with the Accounting department to manage inventory and calculate food and labour costs, but we do not have a dedicated Food and Beverage Controller. We are also supported by a very understanding Human Resources Department.

Q: Approximately how many different products do you need to have in inventory to produce offered standard menu items?
Do you put emphasis on cross utilization and how do you deal with dead stock?
A: We often have groups that come from all over the world to stay with us for extended periods of time. In order to keep people stimulated, we have a ten-day rotational menu that draws from global influences with a focus on using local product. All in all, our inventory consists of over a thousand items with as many as 700 in-stock items at any one time. With menu changes, we inevitably ends up with dead stock, which can be dealt with a number of ways. The first is to avoid it in the first place by tight purchasing that does not affect the team's ability to produce but also does not result in excess. When dead stock occurs in spite of this proactive approach, we can customize menus to use products that are no longer on the regular rotation. In some cases we create specials or use items in our extensive staff cafeteria.

Q: How do you manage purchasing of various products? Do your product needs warrant the 100-mile rule of purchasing and are you concerned about the carbon footprint?
A: We use a combination of one-stop shopping and quotes. For example, for dry goods we work with a single vendor and have negotiated an arrangement based on mark up that we can audit and verify. For some other items, like proteins and produce, we use a quote system. Ultimately minimizing the carbon footprint we make is very important to us. That's why we have as few trucks coming to our door as possible. I work with our produce and meat vendors to source and prioritize local product so that we have the best of both worlds—local product and a minimum number of trucks at the door.

Q: What are your thoughts during the process of creating new (other than seasonal) menu items? i.e., what and why, including preparation challenges (staff, equipment), product/purchasing considerations, plate presentation, and service challenges, i.e., tableside preparation/space requirements…?
A: The first consideration when creating a new menu is to answer "What does the guest want?" I ascertain this by meeting with guests and asking the front of house and the sales department for their feedback before even starting to write. Now that I have a general idea of the direction I want to go, I take many things into account, such as staffing requirements, equipment, flow of production both in prep and service, variety, nutrition, and whether it be done with local product. I even take into account if I can write a good story about this item because for each menu item on the dinner menu I have a one or two sentence story to go along with it. When it comes to actually writing the menu, I do this in collaboration with my team. They will often think of things that I don't or offer ideas on how to do things differently.

Q: How do you and in what way do you consider your customers while creating a menu item description?
How do you deal with the impact of demographic changes?
A: Our guests are often here for days at a time during their conference, so I need to consider their need for a healthy diet and their need for variety.

The Kingbridge Centre is a conference facility and as such the demographic can change from group to group. This is taken into account when creating special menus for that group.

Q: Do you adhere to a standard process (self-imposed or other) in creating a printable menu item description?
A: When writing menus, I try to strike a balance between giving an adequate description of the dish and not becoming overly wordy. Once I have the menu written, I give it to a broad cross section of Kingbridge community members to proofread it and offer feedback before final printing, which is done in house.

Q: Which one of the following most common methods to calculate a menu selling price is your favourite?
Gross profit method. What the market will bear. Cost plus pricing. One selling price method (per menu segment). Psychological and/or Prestige pricing. Variable Cost pricing. Prime Cost pricing. All and/or actual cost pricing. Or do you use a method that is not listed?
A: I receive a daily allocation or (daily food revenue per guest) from which to produce Breakfast, AM Break, Lunch, PM Break, and Dinner. Therefore, on the one hand I'm fortunate that except for banquets I don't really have to price things individually to sell them. On the other hand, I need to cost out an extensive set of possibilities of product that the guests will consume on average on a given day.

For pricing I use a combination of methods here at the Kingbridge Centre. Generally, I do a combined product and labour cost for a group of items such as a breakfast buffet average dinner. I use market data only as a reference point to ensure we stay competitive.

Q: If your staff would ask you what in your opinions is a good food cost percentage for your type of establishment, what would you tell them?
A: This is a very sensitive question and one that I'm not going to answer directly, but I will say the budgeted cost percentage is decided by the chef in collaboration with the leadership team to come up with a number that will yield an acceptable profit and also allow the production of the best possible product within a given price point. Generally. it is about 30%.

Q: Do you like to follow, or have a need and demand to follow, trends?
A: Sometimes there is a need to follow trends. Trends create desires in guests, and I need to place the guests' needs ahead of my own ego. I personally enjoy putting new spins on old classics.

Q: What influences you when making a selection of tableware to complement the food presentation as well as the atmosphere of the establishment?
A: How that piece fits the architecture or the environment of the room, the feel or look of a piece, and how well it will go with other pieces. There are practical considerations as well, like cost, durability, and replacement availability.

Q: Your thoughts about seasonal menu items, impact on slow food, 100-mile menu, and carbon footprint?
A: Sometimes it's hard to build seasonality into menus in Canada in February but there are ways. I think it's important to make menus as seasonal as possible while still providing a wide selection of products to guests. There are very practical reasons for being seasonal such as pricing.

Carbon footprints can be very hard to trace. I reference Canada's seafood sustainability guide and work our regular vendors to connect them with local growers and producers so that I can buy local product without bringing additional trucks to my door.

Q: How frequently do you monitor the performance of offered menu items? Do you use a specific software or system to accomplish this task?
A: I monitor the performance of menu items constantly, if an item is not being received well, I try to find out why, and if I have to change it I do and quickly.

I use our point of sale system (POS), but more so than this, I simply talk to the front of house staff; they will often give me the heads-up on an item long before I think to run a report.

Q: What is your perception of and what do you expect from a "perfect menu"?
A: I think the perfect menu represents first a great experience to the guest, it represents good value to the guest, and it represents a reasonable profit to the operator.

Q: Are there any other thoughts you have on menu planning for today's customer that you would like to share with readers?
A: Know your customers, talk to your customers. Plan menus that meet and exceed their needs and desires, and they will be back. Constantly revisit what and how you do things, collaborate with every member of your team to find efficiencies and for ideas.

For the most recent Kingbridge Conference Centre and Institute menu offerings please visit:

www.kingbridgecentre.com/index.php?option=com_content&view=article&id=79&Itemid=102

Hilde Zimmer,

Photo courtesy of Hilde Zimmer.

Chair, School of Hospitality and Tourism Management
Centre for Hospitality and Culinary Arts
George Brown College
Toronto, Ontario, Canada

Restaurant Menu Likes and Dislikes- A Personal Rant

In many cases, a restaurant's menu is the anchor for a diner's first impression of a restaurant. Whether it's read on a chalkboard advertising the daily catch, a stylish one-pager that takes two hands to hold, or a plastic-coated multi-page booklet complete with photos, grease, and ketchup stains, the restaurant menu is where the customer focuses his eye, his appetite and ultimately, his hard-earned dollars!

To that end, while each dining establishment needs to pay attention to the particular clientele that it is catering to, there are elements to menu presentation and development that should be inherent in each:

- Legibility
- Clarity
- Affordability commensurate with the type of food and beverage offered
- Some novelty (a special for that establishment)
- Some seasonality (don't advertise fresh raspberries when you don't have any!)
- No ripped pages, crossing out, tape, etc., over items no longer available. Respect the customer enough to refresh the menu.I If the menu is old and ragged, what can you expect from the food?

I'm sure this list could grow but for me, those are the items that are top of mind.

The menu is enhanced by the server.

Whether you're greeted with "Hi Guys!," "Good Evening," or "Hello, My name is Gus and I'm your waiter this evening," this first contact should come with a smile that is unhurried, genuine, and eager to please. When asked for details on a particular dish, the answers should be clear, accurate, and either supporting my choice or sending me to another item on the menu. I don't mind being up-sold if it's done with finesse. As I peruse my menu, moving from appetizer to dessert, it's nice to have a well-trained server guiding me with hints of the delights to come should I choose the Flourless Chocolate Torte instead of the Meringue with Seasonal Berries and Cream. For fine dining, the menu can be long and lean, elegantly folded, or perhaps advertised on an iPAD docked on the table. What adds to my enjoyment is an experienced server who can bring the dishes to life as my order is taken, then served with polish and attention to the smallest detail.

For dinner and a movie dining, we go to the multi-pager menu at the bigger chains. It would be really nice to have the actual dish look like the picture depicted on the menu. That's branding for me and I have a favourite steak house that always delivers. What you see is what you should get!

Then there is the neighbourhood diner, with the daily special written in black marker on a whiteboard. The place is packed every noon hour. No fancy menus here, just good simple food and plenty of it. The menu? Still has Hot Beef, Hot Chicken, and Hot Turkey sandwiches and is a simple fold over, black and white, four pages. It has what I would expect coming through the doors, and most people who eat here have the menu memorized and come in for their favourite special of the day or the hamburger that never fails to meet expectations of freshness and taste.

To conclude, the most disappointing menu is the one that pretends to be more than it actually is. Fine print, layout, and advertising may bring a customer in once, but if the quality of the food listed is not available, consistent, and properly presented and served, customers will not return and the business might fail. Making it in a competitive market beyond break even to profitability requires skill in menu design, food preparation, respect for your clientele, and a strong focus on service. A well-presented clear menu that promises consistent quality and freshness for its target clientele is a first step to continued success.

Appendix: Useful Terms for Menu Planning

Chapter 10

The Good, the Not-So-Good and the Bad words in Menu Writing (Author's Opinion)

THE GOOD	THE NOT-SO-GOOD	THE BAD
Aged (Beef, Game, Wine)	A la (unless appropriate)	Accented
Al dente	And (use sparingly)	Accompanied (by/with)
Alternative selection	Any style	Any abbreviation (w/ &)
Aromatic	Authentic (it must be true)	Appetizing
Authentic (if it's true)	Baby (if unavoidable)	Arranged
Bite size	Bland	Assorted
Blend, blended	Chunks-chunky	BBQ
Bouquet	Composed-combined	Bed (on a, in a, under)
Brand descriptor (Tabasco)	Concocted-Concoction	Bountiful
Candied	Cooked in	Coated with
Chilled	Cuts (Macédoine, Brunoise)	Complemented
Classic	Dash	Composed
Coated, Covered	Delectable	Covered, with, covering,
Colour descriptors	Delicate	Crowned
Consistency described (light)	Delicious	Dainty
Cooking methods (any & all)	Deluxe	Dazzle-dazzling
Creamy-smooth	Devine	Delightful
Crisp(y)	Dipped, drippings, dressing	Drenched, Dunked
Cuts (Julienne, sliver, thin)	Dollop	Either, or
Decadent	Drizzled	Embellished
Delicacy	Enveloped	Embraced
Enriched	Exceptional-ly	Encircled-enclosed
Essence	Exotic (if not)	Enhanced

Flaky	Exquisite	Escorted
Folded-wrapped	Favourite (yours, mine)	Extra (everything)
Fragrant	Fancy (unless grade)	Fluffy
Free range (if it's true)	Filled with	Fresh (freshest)
Freshly (squeezed)	Fine, finest	Full flavoured
Fused-infused-fusion of	Finished (with)	Gathered-Gathering
Glazed	Flavoured	Gigantic
Golden (yellow-brown)	Flavourful	Good value
Grass fed (if it's true)	Garnished (try not to use)	Gourmet
Herbed	Gently	Gracious
Hint	Home Style-Homemade	Gratifying
Imported (from where)	In harmony	Heaped-helping
Hot (steaming/burning hot)	Hot from the oven	Heart warming
Marinated in/with	Irresistible	In a dressing, emulsion, jus
Market or Garden fresh	Jumbo (unless Shrimp)	Incredible
Meatless	Layered	Liberal (i.e. serving)
Mild, Spicy	Mature	Luscious-lush
Napped	Nutritious (unless explained)	Luxurious
Organic (if it's true)	Old fashioned	Marvellous
Origin descriptor (i.e. Canadian)	Our very own	Mixture
Original (must be true)	Piping hot	Moistened
Paired	Pleasing	Mound
Piquant	Plump	Mouth-watering
Product type descriptor	Rich	Nested
Reduction-reduced in/with	Scrumptious	On (a) anything
Refreshing	Stuffed with	Overflowing
Robust	Tenderized	Palatable
Rolled	Tidbit	Perfect
Savoury	To perfection (subjective)	Pivoted
Scented	To your liking-order	Placed
Seasonal-in season	Topped	Pleasant-pleasing
Selected	Ultimate	Plenty
Silky	Unusual	Puddle
Sizzling	With (use sparingly)	Quaint
Slow-cooked		Secret (Ingredient, Recipe)

Smoked (hot-cold)		Sensational
Smoked (type of wood)		Served in: Gravy, Dressing
Soft		Served with-on
Style (in reference to)		Smothered
Sumptuous-Succulent		Sprinkled with-on
Sun dried-ripened		Superb
Tantalizing		Surrounded with-by
Tangy		Symphony
Tender		Tantalizing
Traditional (if it is)		Tasty-tasteful
Tropical		To die for
Unique (if it is)		To your liking
Vine ripened		Towering
Wrapped		Wonderful
		Young
Zesty		Zippy
ADD YOUR OWN WORDS:		

If you have any suggestions for "in or exclusions," please send them to etservice1978@gmail.com Thank you!

Menu-planning-related Terms One Might Need to Know

Asian cuisine	Originated as **East Asian** in Imperial China and including Japan and Korea, **Southeast Asian** including Cambodia, India, Sri Lanka, and Pakistan. **Central Asia** including Kazakh, Mongolian, and Uzbek cuisine are not yet as popular and established as **East Asian** cuisine, which includes Cantonese and Shanghai cuisine.
Cajun & Creole cuisine	South Louisiana features two unique cuisines: Creole and Cajun. Cajun cuisine is hearty and robust, featuring strongly seasoned, pungent-flavoured seafood, in pot-cooked meats, and game dishes. Creole cuisine, being European influenced (France and Spain), is more refined in its offerings, featuring several courses in succession, with lighter flavours and smaller portions.
Classical cuisine	Cuisine classique is a style of cooking based on Auguste Escoffier's documented records, which are a refinement of his predecessors Antoine Carême, Jules Gouffê, and Urbain François Dubois methods.

Comfort food	This term was first used in the Webster dictionary in 1977 and refers to food that has the ability to change the emotional status of a consumer. Food items are usually homestyle cooked, and are well-known and liked by the consumer.
Fusion cuisine	This term is used for the combination of various forms of cookery. A common method is regional fusion that combines different cuisines of a region or sub-region into a single food presentation/combination. There are two popular approaches: the eclectic approach, and over-arching fusion. In the 1960s Richard Wing, while working at the Imperial Dynasty Restaurant, **combined French and Chinese cooking** and herewith created Fusion Cuisine. **Wolfgang Puck** is considered as one of the pioneers of fusion cuisine while operating his restaurant Chinois.
Mediterranean cuisine	A cuisine describing the blend of, or the singular usage of, food products and cooking philosophies from the following countries or regions adjacent to the Mediterranean Sea: Greece, Italy–Sardinia & Sicily, Portugal, Catalonia (Mountain), Turkey, France, Israel, Middle Eastern States, Alger, North Africa, Egypt, Iraq, Spain & Valencia, Jordan, Libya, Lebanon, Macedonia, Malta, Syria, Montenegro, Morocco, Palestine, Serbia, Slovenia, and Tunisia.
Menu engineering	A manual or computerised method of analysing the performance of menu items based on menu mix and gross profit/contribution margin. This method was pioneered and published by Michael L. Kasavana and Donald I. Smith in 1982.
Nouvelle cuisine	Meaning "new cooking," this is a contemporary approach toward classical French cooking that seeks to bring out the natural flavours of foods and substitutes light, low-calorie sauces and stocks for the traditional heavy butter-based and cream-based preparations.
Southwest cuisine	See Fusion cooking. This term is used for Middle-Eastern cuisine that was adapted from West Asian and various other countries.
Tex-Mex cuisine	A term used to describe a regional American cuisine that blends food products indigenous to the United States and the culinary creations of Mexican Americans influenced by the cuisines of Mexico. Tex-Mex is very popular in the southern state of Texas also referred to as **Southwestern** cuisine.

Glossary

Chapter 11

Synopsis of common menu terminology

TERM	SHORT EXPLANATION	PAGE(S)
Institutional menu—meal plan	Similar to cycle menu,often "not for profit" like a hospital, prison,	31
À la carte	Menu offerings based on meal periods are listed in customary eating sequence and all offerings are priced individually. Formal look and feel layout.	26
Semi à la carte	Some of the individually priced offerings may be combinations (menu items served with accompaniments, side-dishes, salad, etc.)	27
Boilerplate	Area on menu reserved for address including city, reservation information, hours of operation, special services: catering, special functions/activities, catering, wheelchair accessibility etc.	42
California type	A less formal appearing, often utilizing graphics, à la carte or semi à la carte menu where all meal periods offerings are on one menu	28
Clip-ons, Add-ons	Additional menu offerings usually located on a reserved space on the menu	42–43
Cross-utilization	One product having several menu applications	41
Cycle	Cyclical, repetitive	30
Demographics	Study of a selected area and its inhabitants	61–63
Depiction	Creating an image in someone's mind using words and/or drawings	5
Descriptive copy	The wording used to describe the menu items, including headings	42
Digital menu/menu board	The digital version of the old-fashioned chalkboard	40
Du jour – today's special	Menu offerings of the day	31

Emphasis areas	Areas the eyes focus on while reading a menu	43
Feasibility study and/or target market analysis	A study to estimate the financial success of an establishment within a demographic area	61
Headings	Names of menu section (Appetizer, Soups, Salads)	47
Hybrid	A mix of static, market, and/or cycle menu items	31
Institutional copy	Mission statement, comfort statement, a summary statement of the philosophy, purpose, and/or history of the establishment	42
Limited menu	A menu with selections limited to its offerings	30
Market menu	Menu based on (domestic) market fresh ingredients, "rhythm of calendar"	
Menu or menu copy	The menu copy, merchandising tool , composed of four sections: Headings – Listing of items – Institutional copy – Boilerplate information	42
Merchandising copy	See Menu or menu copy	42
Nutritional	Menu focusing on the various nutritional needs	
Prix fixe (fixed—set price)	Multi-course menu:set item(s), with possible exchange privileges—fixed priced	28
Set menu	A suggested selection of menu items and/or a custom prepared occasion menu	28
Special	Selected from existing offerings or a new menu item available for a specific time period	50
Special occasion or single use menu	See Set menu	28
Static	Seldom changing (Fast food, Steak houses, ethnic specialty restaurants)	31
Table d'hôte	Multi-course menu – package priced – with suggested item(s) exchange privileges –selling price may change with type of package selected	28